101
HAND PUPPETS

A Beginner's Guide to Puppeteering

Richard Cummings

DOVER PUBLICATIONS, INC.
Mineola, New York

Published in the United Kingdom by David & Charles, Brunel House, Forde Close, Newton Abbot, Devon TQ12 4PU.

Bibliographical Note

This Dover edition, first published in 2002, is an unabridged republication of *101 Hand Puppets: A Guide for Puppeteers of All Ages,* originally published by David McKay, Inc., New York, 1962.

Library of Congress Cataloging-in-Publication Data

101 Hand Puppets
p. cm.
Summary: Provides instructions for making and using instant puppets, rainy day puppets, professional puppets, and novelty puppets.
ISBN 0-486-42315-8 (pbk.)
1. Puppets–Juvenile literature. 2. Puppet Making–Juvenile literature.
[1. Puppets. 2. Puppet making. 3. Handicraft.]

PN1972 .G25
791.5'3—dc21

2002025918

Manufactured in the United States of America
Dover Publications, Inc., 31 East 2nd Street, Mineola, N.Y. 11501

This book is for
DIANA

"GEORGE SAND developed very decided theories about the little dolls ... Her feeling was that when she thrust her hand into the empty skirt of the inanimate puppet it became alive with her soul in its body, the operator and the puppet completely one."

HELEN HAIMAN JOSEPH
A Book of Marionettes

Your Puppets Are You

HERE ARE one hundred and one puppets for you. The list begins with a handkerchief puppet that you can make with a twist of the wrist, and ends with a modern version of the giant and elaborate puppets of Osaka, Japan. Some of the ideas are brand-new; some are as old as history. If you were to construct and operate them all, you could consider yourself a master puppeteer. On the other hand, you will come to know, as every good puppeteer does, that the simplest puppet is often the best.

There are plays too, and designs for stages and props, suggestions on performance, and detailed instructions on the use of materials—all of which can be quickly located through the index at the back.

Choose a puppet, gather your materials, and begin. Watch your puppet take life under your hands. Slip him on, turn him this way and that, cause him to speak, to laugh, to think—he will delight you; he might even surprise you.

The famous lady writer, George Sand, was a puppet fan. "Her feeling was that when she thrust her hand into the empty skirt of the inanimate puppet it became alive with

her soul in its body, the operator and the puppet completely one."

It's true. Your puppets will lead you into a new and
wondrous world from which you will not—cannot escape.
It is, after all, the world of yourself.

Contents

The Puppets

INSTANT PUPPETS

1. Instant Bunny
2. Thumbelina
3. Winkums
4. Jabberwacky
5. Bagdad, Paper-bag Gremlin
6. Beaknik, Envelope Bird
7. Matchbox Monster
8. Spoonerella
9. Rapid Rabbit
10. Spook-a-boo the Ghost
11. Carrie Carrot
12. Turnip the Tusker
13. The Apple Pirate
14. Eggbert
15. Borrowed Hedda
16. Plasticman

RAINY DAY PUPPETS

17. Little Miss Muffet
18. The Spider
19. Goldilocks
20. Papa Bear
21. Mama Bear
22. Baby Bear
23. Robert Robot
24. Stocking Dragon
25. Perky Pup
26. Old Joe Crow
27. Maccus the Jester
28. Harlequin

PROFESSIONAL PUPPETS

SPECIAL PUPPETS

NOVELTY PUPPETS

101
HAND PUPPETS

A Beginner's Guide to Puppeteering

Instant Puppets

THESE PUPPETS can be made—well, nearly—in an instant. They call for materials that you are sure to have handy, such as handkerchiefs, lipstick, matchboxes, salad spoons and right and left hands. Have a minute? Try one.

1. INSTANT BUNNY

You need a large handkerchief. Make a loose fist and drape the handkerchief over it, as shown in diagram A. With your other hand, pull one of the front corners of the handkerchief up between your first two fingers. That's one ear. Now do the same with the other corner, pulling it up between the second and third fingers. Two ears. Wrap the two back corners around your wrist, and you have a bunny with floppy ears and a wriggly nose (your second finger inside the handkerchief).

2. THUMBELINA

With a ball-point pen draw a funny face on your thumb and drape a handkerchief over it, as in B. Pull it around in front to hide your hand. You can also put a peanut shell on your thumb and draw Thumbelina's peek-a-boo face on that.

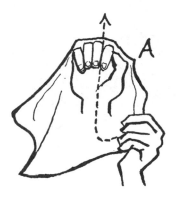

A

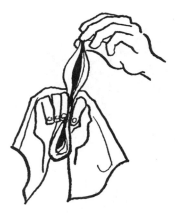

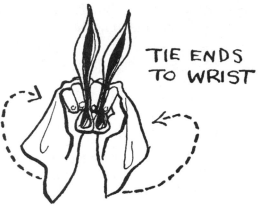

TIE ENDS
TO WRIST

B

3. WINKUMS

Find the fold in the palm of your hand—just under the little finger. Draw one eye right on that fold. Draw the rest of the face to fit, as in C. Now, by curling your little finger down you make Winkums wink, wink, WINK!

4. JABBERWACKY

With your ball-point pen draw a face on the back of your hand, as shown, D. Use a lipstick to color the lower half of your first finger and the upper part of your thumb. Now make a fist. Your first finger becomes the upper part of the mouth, your thumb the lower part, and by moving them you can make Jabberwacky talk, whistle and even pretend to chew gum.

Riddles for Jabberwacky

Now to produce a little play. You ask riddles and Jabber gives the answers. Like this:

YOU: What is it that a cat has that no other animal has?

JABBER: Kittens.

YOU: Why does an Indian wear a feather headdress?

JABBER: To keep his wig wam.

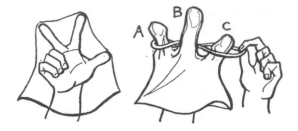

An Instant Body

To make a quick body or "skirt" you need a large handkerchief and a rubber band. Hold your hand in one of the two hand positions shown below and drape the handkerchief over the extended fingers. Loop the rubber band over the handkerchief and around finger, A. Pull it around back of finger, B. Finally, loop it over your thumb, C. The head is placed on the first finger, and the thumb and the other finger become the puppet's arms.

The Hand Positions

Below are two ways of holding your hand inside a puppet. The first one gives the puppet's arms a longer reach and a better grip on props, but it tends to tilt the puppet to one side. The second position is more balanced, but the little finger makes a shorter arm. It is harder to get it and the thumb together to hold on to props. The first position is the one most commonly used and the best for small hands.

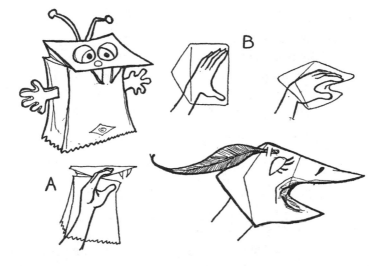

5. BAGDAD THE PAPER-BAG GREMLIN

You need crayons, scissors and a small brown paper grocery bag. Flatten the bag out and turn it with the open side down. The fold across the top will be Bagdad's mouth and should be marked with a line of bright red. Cut out two white paper fangs and paste them to the edge of the fold, pointing downward. Now draw a button nose and two big droopy eyes above the mouth. Add paper feelers on top if you wish. Put your hand inside the bag and fit your fingers into the flap, as in A. You will find that by opening and closing your hand you can make Bagdad's mouth open and close. This gremlin speaks English, and he loves to sing.

6. BEAKNIK THE ENVELOPE BIRD

You need an envelope and crayons. Put your hand inside the envelope, B, stretching your fingers into the upper corner and your thumb into the lower. With your other hand press in the front edge of the envelope. Pull it away quickly or it will be nipped, for by opening and closing the hand inside the envelope, you make Beaknik's beak open and shut. Add an eye, fierce or friendly, according to taste.

7. THE MATCHBOX MONSTER

You need a wooden matchbox, some colored paper and glue. Throw away the drawer part of the matchbox. Cover the outside of the other part with paper (light blue is nice and monsterly). Cut out two circles of colored paper, one smaller than the other. Cut the circles in half and use a half of each to form each eye, as shown. Cut out a fringe of black hair and two goofy teeth. Glue the features in place. With match stubs or glass tacks you can make the electrodes that this monster has instead of ears (where he plugs in when his battery is down). Make an instant body for him and slip the matchbox head down over the first finger. And now, beware of the Franklystern Monster!

8. SPOONERELLA

You need a large wooden salad spoon, crayons and one of the scouring pads made of woven copper or brass foil. Draw a face on the back or rounded part of the spoon. If you wish, you can paste on paper features. Spread the center of the scouring pad with your thumbs and slip it on over the top of the spoon to make a crown of shiny hair. Now grip the spoon in your hand as shown. Drape a bright handkerchief over the extended thumb and finger and *in front of your hand.* Secure it with a rubber band the way you did with the instant body, except that in this case the rubber band runs around behind the spoon handle instead of behind your first finger.

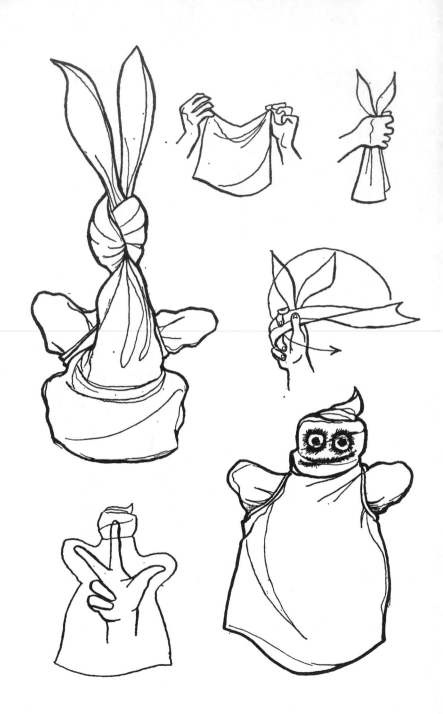

9. RAPID RABBIT

Quick like a bunny, find a large white handkerchief and a rubber band. Lift two corners of the handkerchief to form two ears and grasp it as shown. Now bring the bottom end of the handkerchief up and around the base of the ears. Make a knot, leaving the ears sticking up. The knot is the rabbit's head. Work your first finger into the knot to hold the head upright, hiding your hand behind the drape of the handkerchief. Use the drape and your rubber band to complete the rabbit with an instant body.

10. SPOOK-A-BOO THE GHOST

Once more you need the handkerchief and the rubber band. Tie a knot in one corner of the handkerchief. Push the knot around until you have a surface on which to draw a face in crayon or ink. Make an instant body out of the hanging part of the handkerchief, and you have a spooky guest for your next Halloween party.

Making Your Puppets Move

Manipulation, or making puppets move, is not so easy as it might seem. At first you are likely to move them too much and too rapidly. Remember that your puppets are small. Their movements should be small and precise. The great advantage of hand puppets over marionettes is that they are truly alive—there is a *living hand* inside. So it is all right for them to stand still now and then, because they always vibrate with life. In front of a mirror practice every kind of movement—a questioning tilt of the head, a shrinking away in fright, a slow suspicious swing of the nose.

11. CARRIE CARROT

She is made from a fat carrot with the big end up. Her nose can be a colored thumb tack, a glass tack or a button held in place by a pin. Cut her eyes out of paper and pin them on. Make her lips from paper or a bit of orange slice. Use a scouring pad for hair. For her skirt, grip the carrot as you did the salad spoon and drape an instant body.

12. TURNIP THE TUSKER

Find a turnip with a long, curled-up end like an elephant's trunk. With an apple-corer bore a hole in the bottom for your first finger. Add thumb tack eyes, round paper ears and toothpick tusks.

13. THE APPLE PIRATE

Bore a hole in the bottom of a shiny apple for your finger. Pin on a mustache of black paper and a black eye patch. Add a cardboard ear with a notebook paper reinforcement for an earring. Tie a bright bit of cloth around the top of the head. Use a bright handkerchief for the pirate's instant body.

14. EGGBERT

Bore a small hole in one end of a fresh egg and a larger hole in the other end. Blow through the smaller hole, and the inside of the egg will push out. Now you can paint a face with water colors and add a piece of fuzzy cloth for hair. Carefully enlarge the neck hole and slip Eggbert on your first finger.

15. BORROWED HEDDA

The heads of old rubber toys and dolls make good instant puppet heads. Sometimes the head has to be stuffed with cotton to let you hold your first finger tightly inside.

16. PLASTICMAN

Model a head from plasticine or modeling clay, with a snug hole in the neck for your first finger. Here is a man of many faces, for with a pinch of your fingers you can flatten his nose or lengthen it or remove it altogether.

A

B

C

Instant Stages

By now you have your hands full of puppets. How about a stage? It won't take long to tack a sheet across a doorway, as in A. Make sure it is high enough to hide your head, but not so high that it hides the puppets you hold up. You can drape the same sheet over the front of a table and lift your puppets from a kneeling position behind the table, B. Or wear a big apron, C. Its corners can be lifted by two fellow puppeteers—in just one instant.

Rainy Day Puppets

HERE IS A WAY to fill a rainy day with fun: make a puppet and give a little show. Most of the materials you will need are around the house. Glue, poster paint, colored paper, rags, yarn, old socks—do you have them? Then, let's go!

17. LITTLE MISS MUFFET

You need yarn, a bit of lace or rickrack, construction paper, a bathroom tissue tube or paper towel tube and an old glove. Cut a 3-inch section of the tube (3½ inches if you are using paper towel tube). Make another tube of stiff paper big enough to fit snugly over the top of your first finger, but *too tight to slip down past the second joint of the finger.* Insert this tube into the larger one and glue it in place with no more than an inch sticking out. Cut the eyes, eyebrows and mouth out of paper and glue them in place. Make three coils of yellow yarn. Tie them together as shown. Glue them in place on top of the tube face. Miss Muffet needs a glove body with a bit of rickrack or lace sewed to the palm to give her a flouncy look.

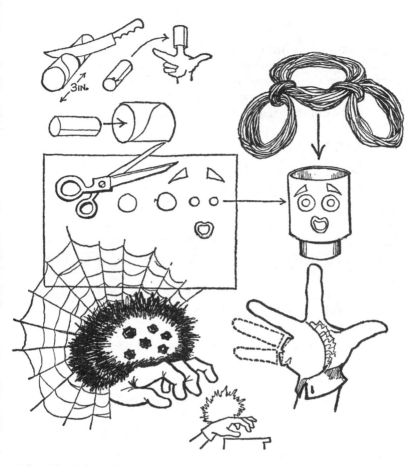

18. THE SPIDER

Sew or glue an old piece of fur to the back of a glove. Glue six shiny black buttons into the fur for eyes. Crouch your fingers to make the awful creature scuttle up behind Miss Muffet.

A Glove Body

To make a quick body out of an old glove, just tuck the

fingers you are not using out of sight. Or you can cut the
spare fingers off and sew up the holes. You will need a glove
large enough to allow you to double your fingers up inside.
Hands of cardboard, as described on page 22, can be slipped
over the ends of the second finger and thumb.

19. GOLDILOCKS

Paper heads are fun and fast to make with construction
paper and glue. On pink construction paper draw out the
large shape, A, about twice the size shown. Cut out along
the solid outside line. (The features are shown only to
show you where to glue them.) Bend this piece around,
overlap and glue at dotted line to make the basic head
shape.

Now copy out the features and cut them out: lips, B;
nose, C; and eyelids, D. Light blue paper is good for the
eyelids, pink for the nose, red for the lips, yellow for the
hair. Bend the two little tabs of each eyelid *under* and glue
them in position, not perfectly flat, but cupped outward
like a real eyelid. Eyes and eyebrows can be painted on
or also cut out and glued. Lips and nose are glued on in
the same way.

Braid the long side tabs of the hair piece, E, and curl
the bangs so that they fall over the forehead when the
piece is glued on top of the head shape. (Crepe paper is
best for this wig.) Roll the neck piece, F, around your
first finger so that it fits snugly down to the second joint,
then glue. When it is dry, glue it up inside and against
the back of the head shape to form the neck. Roll and fit
the hands, G, to fit your thumb and little finger. Use an
instant body, a glove body, or the simple puppet skirt
described on page 22. You can use this same basic head
shape and method for any other human character you wish
to make.

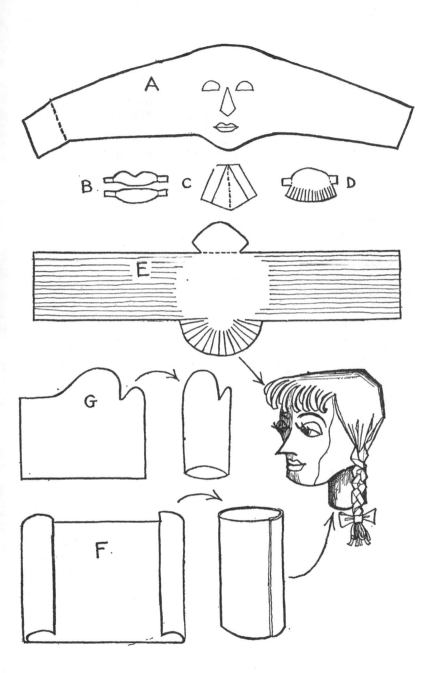

20. PAPA BEAR

Make the gruff old bruin exactly as you made Goldilocks, using the basic head shape shown, A. The features are glued on in the same way: eyelids (for Mama Bear), nose, neck piece. Cup the ears, B, forward when gluing them in position. Paint eyes and frowning eyebrows. A straw hat can be added, if you wish, C.

21. MAMA BEAR

Her basic head shape might be a bit smaller than Papa's. She need not have such a fierce frown. Add a pink bow between her ears and an apron to her dress to give her that feminine look.

22. BABY BEAR

He's just a little fellow, of course, but made just like his papa. He can wear a beanie of crepe paper. The bodies of all three bears can be made of brown paper, wool, felt or actual fur. Their paws, D, are made just like Goldilock's hands.

A Ready-Made Play

Now you have all the characters you need for a complete play about Goldilocks and the Three Bears. There is no need to write out a script; everybody knows the story. Just go through it once or twice, talking it out as you go along and having fun until you are ready to present it to a little group of friends or parents. In this way you can make plays out of many other folk tales and nursery rhymes that we all know; *Sleeping Beauty* for instance. (The Prince would have the same basic head shape as Goldilocks, but without the braids!)

23. ROBERT ROBOT

Here's a goggle-eyed, gleaming monster made out of a tissue tube and aluminum foil. Construct his head as you did Miss Muffet's (No. 17), then wrap it in aluminum foil. By pinching and pushing the foil this way and that you can get the most gruesome features. Cut the large parts of the eyes from paper and stick them to the head with silver-headed thumb tacks, which then make the pupils of the eyes.

Rainy Day Hands

Robert's right hand can be cut from foil in the shape shown, A, which is then fitted around the little finger, overlapped and glued or pinched in place. For his left hand, fit the same shape to the thumb. Simpler mitten hands can be made from paper or foil as for Goldilocks (No. 19). Longer lasting wrap-around hands, as in A, can be made of felt, leather or cardboard. Soft wire twisted in the shape shown, B, can be covered with cloth or paper and then fitted to a paper or leather cuff.

The Basic Body

Here is the pattern, C, for the basic puppet skirt or body. Two pieces are cut and sewed together down the sides, leaving neck, wrists and hem open. You will have to experiment to get the proper size for your hand, large enough to allow free movement, but not so large that too much material gets in your way. Once you have discovered the right size, make a pattern of cardboard and keep it.

With a little experimentation you will discover ways of padding out your skirts to make characters fat or broadshouldered or bosomy. The method shown (D) has the hands attached by rubber bands to a little pillow, which fits in the palm of your hand under the skirt. This has the advantage of also holding the hands firmly in place on thumb and little finger.

24. STOCKING DRAGON

Make sure the stocking is clean and the color you want.
Green for dragons? Thrust your hand inside the sock, as
shown, keeping the fingers together to form the upper part
of the mouth, the thumb lowered to form the lower jaw.
Poke the toe of the stocking back into your hand to form
the mouth. Sew across the fold at each corner of the mouth
to hold it in place. The mouth can now be lined with red
cloth or felt. A tongue, forked, flat or flappy can be added.
Because your thumb is not in the center of your hand, you
might want to add wadded cloth or felt stiffening beside
it to keep it in balance. You will find that with a little practice you can make the flexible mouth grin comically, smirk
and turn down grumpily. Eyes are buttons on discs of
paper or felt. The dragon's crest is cut from felt and sewed
along his spine, which is the back of your hand and wrist.

25. THE PERKY PUP

Use a brown or black or speckled stocking and add the
pup's floppy felt ears. For droopy eyes, first sew on bright
black buttons, then cup a half circle of felt over them and
sew it down. For a nose add a little bulb of black cloth
or a big button.

26. OLD JOE CROW

This bird has a bill of cardboard in two parts. The sock
is first prepared as before, with the folds at the corners
wrapped, then the upper and lower bills are glued in
place. Use quick-drying household cement and glue the
bill on with your hand inside the sock, holding it firmly
in place until dry. For eyes, use buttons, sequins or the
eyes used on stuffed toys.

27. MACCUS THE JESTER

Here is a simple animated head named after the Roman god Maccus, ancestor of the most famous puppet of all, Mr. Punch, (No. 38). Cut the two pieces from stiff cardboard and paint them white on one side. Hinge the jaw as shown with a brass paper holder, loose rivet or small nut and bolt. Attach the control wire to the back end of the jaw, using wire that is stiff enough to give good control. Attach a stick to the head, making sure it does not interfere with the jaw movement. Now paint the features. Maccus can cackle, jabber and sing. There's only one trouble: he can face in only one direction!

28. HARLEQUIN

Here is the father of all clowns and another ancestor of Mr. Punch. He is assembled just as Maccus was: all five parts of stiff cardboard or thin wood; hinges loose enough to allow free movement; stick placed so as not to interfere with movement; control wire stiff for good control. (Coathanger wire is a little heavy, but stiff enough.) Harlequin dances mostly, although he can flag down trains very handily.

29. DANCING BEAR

Rod puppets are discussed amongst other Special Puppets on page 94, but you can make this dancing bear and his ball as easily as you have made Harlequin. In this case there is no holding stick; the control wires hold him upright, so they must be good and stiff. Note also that this time the legs are hinged on the side of the body toward the audience. The bear can waltz, chase his ball, balance on it, or balance it on his nose. One puppeteer can operate the bear, the other the ball; or, with practice, you can operate both yourself.

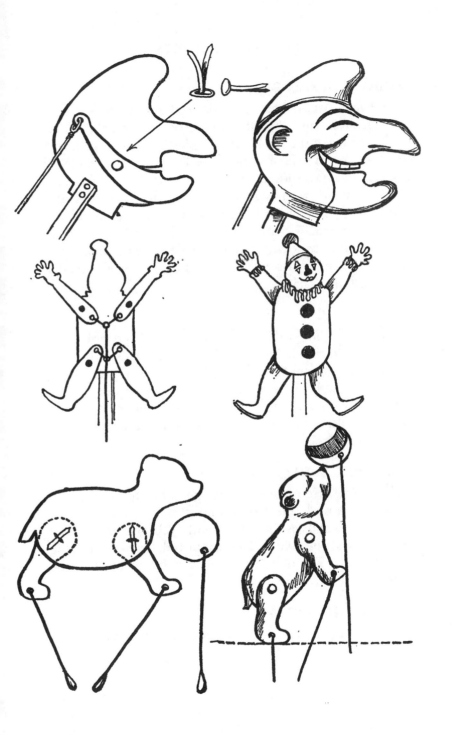

30. BOBO BLOCKHEAD

Bore a finger-sized hole in a block of soft wood such as pine or balsa. Into this fit a finger tube of cardboard or leather to make the neck. Glue a plastic thimble or a red wooden bead in place for the nose. The eyes are two cloth-covered buttons with dots of black ink for pupils. The mouth is made with two cuts of a razor blade or sharp knife. A piece of white toothbrush plastic is glued in for a tooth. Cut ears out of cardboard or balsa and glue them in place. Glue on a wild wig of tangled yarn or just plain straw. Paint him with poster paints or, better yet, model airplane dope.

31. BALDY BALL

You need a hollow rubber ball, unpainted if possible. Cut a hole for your first finger and insert a cardboard finger tube. Rubber cement will help hold it in place, but it should fit snugly. It is best to paint on the features so as to keep the round, baldish effect. Use rubber cement to glue two tufts of cotton over the ears and give him what little hair he has.

32. RAGGEDY RUTHY

Make a little bag of pink or orange cloth, thrust a finger tube into its neck, tie it tight and glue it. Turn the head right side up and sew on a nose and eyebrows of felt. The mouth is best embroidered in bright red. The eyes are big blue buttons. For hair try yarn or a bit of cotton loop rugging.

33. GORDO THE WIZARD

Prepare a small gourd with a neck tube as shown. Paint

the features and wizard's starry cap with enamel or air-plane dope. Add a nose and glasses cut from construction paper.

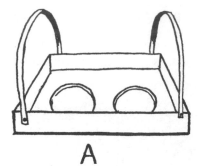

A

B

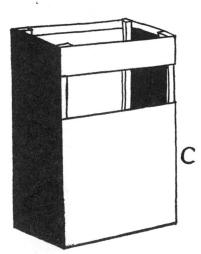

C

Making Up a Play

By now you must have enough puppets to put together a little play of your own. You only need two or three. What if we find Gordo the Wicked Wizard in his laboratory making a mechanical man?—Robert Robot, of course!

Cackling horribly, Gordo presses the button of his infernal machine and brings Robert to life. "Go get me a fair maiden, I command you!" cries the wizard and scampers into his study. Robert looks hopefully about. No fair maidens in sight. But who should wander in just at that moment but Raggedy Ruthy, a maiden anyhow, and fair enough. Robert jumps at her. She screams. They run in circles. A heroic barking is heard. Perky Pup to the rescue! You take it from there. No need to write it down. Just go through it in your mind or talk it over with your partner. Make the story as simple as possible with lots of action, and whatever you do, have fun. That's what puppets are made for.

Rainy Day Stages

A tray stage can be made out of the bottom part of a dress box as shown, A. The table stage, B, is made from a pasteboard box, and fixed to the table so that part of the open bottom juts out to admit the puppets. The larger box stage, C, can be made out of a big pasteboard box or out of cardboard tacked to a wooden frame. The operator kneels inside the open back of the box.

Backgrounds can be painted on cards that fit into the back of the stage and can be quickly changed. Scenery and props, such as trees and furniture, can be attached to the sides of the stage or even placed on the table in front of the stage. Don't worry about a curtain. Everybody knows that when the puppets pop up, the play has begun, and when they pop down, it is over. However, a bow and a thank you at the end do help your audience to know when to applaud.

Professional Puppets

THESE ARE THE puppets for entertaining at school, church and community gatherings. They are durable, but not too difficult to make. They offer you plenty of room to use your imagination, but they are not too complicated for use on a portable stage and under the varied conditions you are liable to run into doing neighborhood shows. They take a little time to make, but still no special skills are required. Seven different methods of making heads are described in this section. Study them all carefully before choosing the one that is best suited to your particular ambition and need.

34. LITTLE RED RIDING HOOD

She wears a red cloak and hood over the basic cloth underskirt. Her hands are of felt sewed over wire frames and fixed to cuffs of cardboard which have been sewed and glued to the sleeves of the underskirt. Her head is made of quick papier-mâché.

Quick Papier-Mâché

A quick papier-mâché head can be made at one sitting of

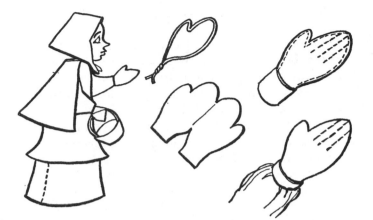

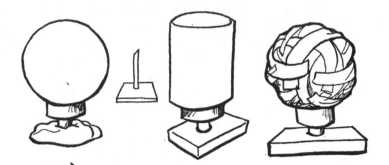

an hour or so, dried overnight and painted the second day. Papier-mâché is cheap, takes paint well and is pretty durable. Its flexibility is an advantage. A plaster or plastic wood head, when banged sharply, might break; a papier-mâché head will only dent and can be repaired. But it does dent easily, whereas it takes quite a crack to break a plastic wood head.

You will need flour, water, salt, newspaper, a prepared head shape and some kind of stand to hold the head upright. For this you can use a store spindle, a three-inch stick thrust into a platform of modeling clay, a small board with a big nail driven through it—anything that will hold the head in position so that you can work on it from all sides.

Prepare a head shape by securing a tight wad of paper around a neck tube with string or paper tape as shown—by fixing a-neck tube to a small rubber ball as was suggested with Baldy Ball (No. 31), or by fixing a neck tube to a toilet tissue tube, as with Miss Muffet (No. 17). Place the head shape in position on the stand. Cut the newspaper into strips of a quarter inch to an inch wide. Pour water into the flour, mixing slowly, until you have a paste about the consistency of thick soup. Mix in a teaspoon of salt. Select one of the wider strips and drag it through the paste, squeezing off the excess between your thumb and forefinger but making sure there is a thin coating of paste on both sides. Lay this around the head shape. Soak another strip with paste and lay it on. Cover the head gradually, making sure the strips overlap at all points and cover it entirely. Add another layer.

Now build up simple features by pinching and adding little wads of saturated paper, which are then overlaid with bits torn from the narrower strips. Remember that most details can be painted on. Concentrate on forming the proper head shape, pinching out a suggestion of the nose and forming the two shallow depressions for eye sockets. Smooth out air bubbles and cover over unwanted pits with little bits of soaked paper. Dry in a warm room on a radiator, in the sun

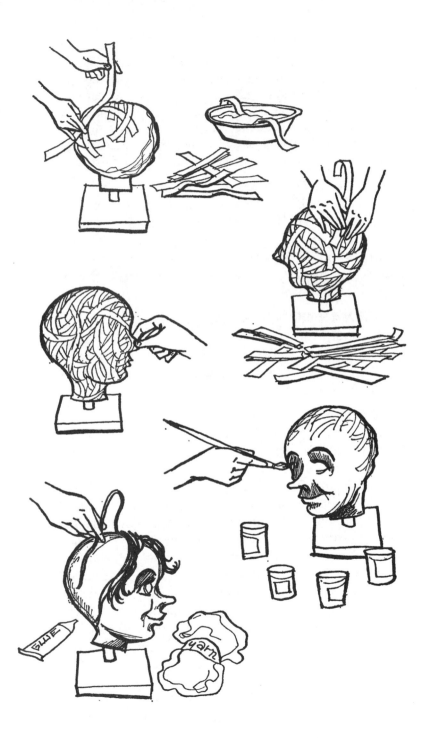

or on the opened door of a low oven. Further repairs can be made the next day if you wish. Paint with poster paints. After the paint is thoroughly dry, you can spray the head with clear plastic from a pressurized can for protection. Red Riding Hood's hair is made from red yarn glued in place strand by strand *after* the paint has thoroughly dried. Details on more advanced use of papier-mâché are given further on.

35. DAME RIDING HOOD

Red's mother wears a blue dress and a white apron over her underskirt. Her hair (which can be made of theatrical crepe hair) barely shows under a tight dustcap. Her bosom is made to billow with the addition of a little roll of padding sewed to the underskirt under her dress. Her head is quick papier-mâché.

36. GOODMAN RIDING HOOD

Red's father, who saves her from the wolf in the end, is a stoutish woodsman. His stomach is the result of padding added to the underskirt under his wide belt. His head is also quick papier-mâché.

37. THE WOLF

"But why have you such big teeth, Grandma?" "Because they are cut from thick cardboard, my dear." So is the mouth, which is cut in two pieces and hinged to fit the hand as shown. Two glued loops of cardboard or tape hold the fingers on top and the thumb below. A big stocking is then cut (on the dotted line) and slipped over the hand. The cut edges of the sock are glued to the edges of the mouth. Cloth ears and button eyes are added, the mouth is painted red and the teeth are glued in place. Arms which can rest outside the covers of Grandma's bed can be made of cloth-covered cardboard and sewed in place. An easier wolf can be made along the lines of the Stocking Dragon (No. 24).

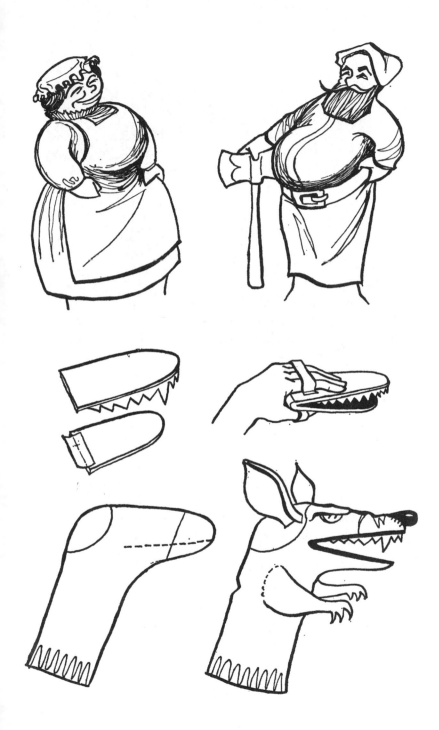

38. PUNCH

He has been known as Pickle Herring, Hanswurst, Kasperle, Polichinelle and Punchinello. Beloved and persecuted in a dozen countries, he has been up to his wicked tricks for hundreds of years and is not likely to stop now, although he might change his name every hundred years or so. Here he is, complete with his poor family and enemies (he has no friends) and his play. Don't be too hard on him for his many sins; after all, he's only a puppet.

> *"Do you know, then, what Polichinelle is? He is the good sense of the people, the brisk sally, the irrepressible laughter. Yes, Polichinelle will laugh and sing as long as the world contains vices, follies and things to ridicule. You see very well that Polichinelle is not near his death. Polichinelle is immortal."*
>
> CHARLES MAGNIN

Modeling in Plasticine

Before we can overcast Punch's head in papier-mâché, we must make a model of plasticine, a re-usable plastic modeling clay available at all art stores. For modeling tools use professional tools or anything handy—spoons, knives, orange sticks. A pound of plasticine will last you through many, many puppets. Make a ball approximately the size of the head you will make, attach a neck and jamb the whole thing down onto a working spindle. Make sure you have the features in balance on the head by beginning with guide lines to indicate the position of the nose and the line of the eyes.

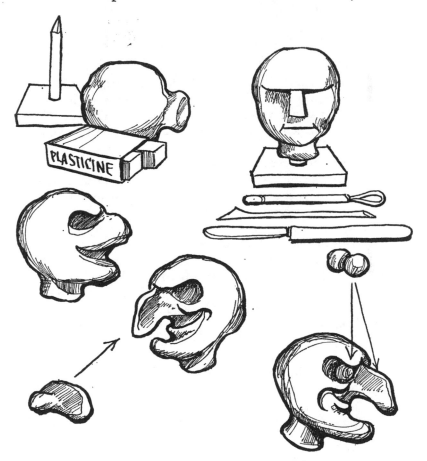

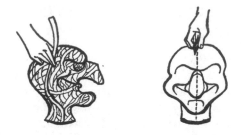

Model the features roughly at first, adding clay where needed, then refine your work. Avoid details such as hair texture and wrinkles, as they will be lost in the overcasting and can be added later. Remember too that many details can be painted on.

Overcasting in Papier-Mâché

Prepare the flour paste as you did for quick papier-mâché. You can add a drop of formaldehyde to drive away any insects that might want to eat your puppets. CAUTION: *formaldehyde is poisonous; do not mix your paste in eating or cooking vessels.* Prepare strips of newspaper as you did for quick papier-mâché. Cover the plasticine head with a very thin coat of vaseline or butter. Lay on the saturated strips carefully, criss-crossing them for strength and making sure the head is completely covered with each coat. Put on at least four coats. More than five will probably obscure the details of the model. You can accentuate features by pinching the papier-mâché shell out a little here and there. You can also add features, such as ears, by building out with wads of the saturated paper and securing these in place with more strips. Use smaller bits for difficult places, such as the tip of the nose and the lips. Dip your fingers in water and lightly smooth down the last coat, making sure there are no air bubbles or unwanted wrinkles.

Dry thoroughly in the sun (48 hours at least) or with a

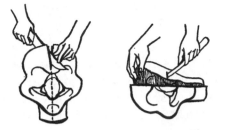

mild artificial heat. Then with a sharp razor blade cut through the shell into the plasticine along the line shown in the diagram, page 40. When the features are not so prominent as Punch's beak nose, you can cut the shell in half sideways, along a line going through each ear. Complete the halving of the head, with a sharp knife, working it carefully down through the clay so as not to crumble the edges of the paper shell. Carefully remove the two halves of the plasticine model from the two halves of the shell, using a dull knife as gouge. Allow the shell halves to dry (do *not* use artificial heat), and then glue them back together to form the hollow head. There will be some warping, and the edges of the shell may not match perfectly. The seam can be smoothed with the addition of more strips of papier-mâché. The bottom of the neck and any small bubbles and unwanted wrinkles can be smoothed down with a razor blade or fine sand paper. Glue a neck tube inside the neck, paint with poster paints or oils, and Punch is ready for his stocking cap and little hump-backed body. His club should be padded with cloth or made of rubber or styrofoam to save damage to the other puppets, his dear family and dear enemies.

39. JUDY

Punch's wife has her husband's great hooked beak and jutting chin, but there is a certain pleasing innocence in her insipid smile and beady eyes. She wears a dress of pale lavender and a little lace cap. Notice that legs of stuffed cloth have been attached to the underskirt and dangle out from beneath her dress. Similar legs can be added to all the characters. They are seldom used for actual walking, but are flopped over the front rim or apron of the stage when the puppets are sitting. Articulated wooden legs for hand puppets are described on pages 120 and 121.

40. THE BABY

This is a little rag doll built over two crossed sticks. (To save time, you could use a store-bought doll.) Make the head out of quick papier-mâché and paint on the yowling mouth. The arms stick straight out to either side; the dress flaps loosely at the end as Master Punch is tossed about by his father.

41. TOBY THE DOG

Toby is the only member of the family who gets a crack at Punch, so he needs good usable jaws for nipping that rascal's nose. He can be a simple stocking puppet (see No. 24), or he can be made like the wolf (No. 37). Front paws of stuffed cloth can be added as shown.

42. SCARAMOUCHE

Scaramouche masquerades here as the mailman, wearing a gray uniform. His head, made of overcast papier-mâché, is not glued to the neck tube, but just fits down over it, so that a sharp blow from Punch's club sends the head flying and leaves the puppeteer's first finger wiggling like a severed neck. You could paint the tip of the finger red, or is that too grisly?

43. PAT THE POLICEMAN

Pat is a jolly fellow, wearing a neat blue uniform. He carries a club, something like Punch's, but it doesn't do him much good.

44. JACK KETCH THE HANGMAN

Jack wears a black mask and black cape. The noose hanging from his gallows tree must be large enough and stiff enough to be easily slipped over *his* head. Single-strand insulated wire is better than cotton cord because it will hold the loop shape.

45. THE GHOST

Make a vague, spooky blue mask of quick papier-mâché, attach it to a twisted wire body with cardboard hands, attach this to a stick and drape some filmy white gauze over the whole thing. He will be frightening enough with his jiggling wire arms and fluttering white shrouds.

46. THE DEVIL

He is a dashing demon, dressed in clashing shades of red, scarlet and tangerine. His pitchfork should be made of wood or tin and be strong enough actually to lift his victim right off the puppeteer's hand and carry him away to Purgatory.

The Swazzle

Traditionally, the shrill inhuman voice of Mr. Punch is produced with the aid of the swazzle or *sifflet-pratique*. It is made of two discs of metal tied together with strips of cloth or tape. In speaking it is held between the tongue and the roof of the mouth, and the voice seems to buzz between the discs, coming out shrill and metallic. It takes some experimentation to make a good swazzle and more experimentation to make it work properly, so unless you have the time for long practice, it can be dispensed with. Besides, during the excitement of Punch's battle with the devil, there is serious danger of swallowing your swazzle!

A Portable Scrim Stage

This is a folding, portable stage for use with professional puppets. It uses a semi-transparent backdrop or "scrim" of heavy gauze or semi-transparent cotton material, hung between the operator and his puppets, A. (See page 78 for the other basic type of puppet presentation, the overhead stage.)

The 3-screen stage should be approximately of the dimensions shown. The framework can be made of wood, aluminum piping or aluminum angle strips. The three frames are pin-hinged together B, so that they can be easily taken apart for transport. A bar across the open back locks the screens into position when in use, C. The masking material, of cloth, canvas or heavy cardboard, D, can be permanently tacked to the frames or can be draped attractively. The playboard, E, should be about six inches wide and placed in the proscenium opening so that half of it is set back inside the stage. This way, properties can be clipped to the back edge of the board while the curtains are closed in front. For the draw curtains, F, use any of the standard drapery tracks. Or the two curtains can be simply hung from eyelets on a wire and drawn by hand from inside. Lighting is best placed outside the proscenium as shown, G. The rod from which the scrim hangs should be movable forward and back. It must be close enough to the playboard so that the puppets can manipulate props placed on the board. Background scenery can be painted on the scrim with poster paint; backgrounds can be varied by the use of any number of removable scrims, each with its supporting rod. The great advantage of this type of stage is that the operator has direct vision of his puppets and props through the scrim. However, it has to be a shallow stage and cannot be much wider than shown here.

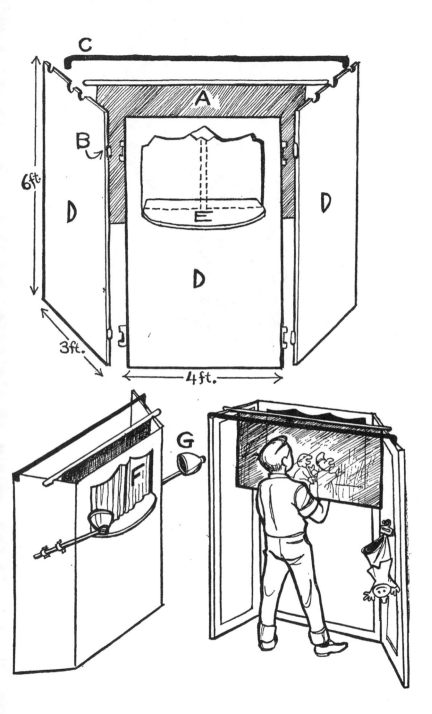

PUNCH AND JUDY

PUNCH AND JUDY

A Tragical Drama for Toys
in One Act

A note on the production: *As there are never more than two puppets on the stage at one time, one performer can do the whole show. The plot of the Punch drama is always pretty much the same, but the dialogue varies according to the taste and invention of the performer. You don't have to use the lines given here. Each of the exchanges can be drawn out as long as you wish it and the audience enjoys it. Punch has always been more cheerfully nonsensical than witty, so don't be afraid to slip in any silly answer or addlepated verse that pops to mind.*

Curtain opens. Punch discovered, peering at audience.

PUNCH: Root-ity-toot-ity-toot, Good morning, good morning! (*He keeps it up until the audience answers.*)

PUNCH: Have you seen my Judy? Oh, she is a beauty! Have you seen my Judy, my root-ily-toot-ily-Judy? (*He keeps it up until the audience answers.*)

PUNCH: No? Then I'll call her. Judy, my dear! Judy!

Enter Judy carrying Baby.

PUNCH: Isn't she a beauty?

JUDY: Well, Mr. Punch, what do you want?

PUNCH: Why, I want to give you a kiss, to be sure. (*Punch reaches for her, misses, kisses the side of the stage noisily.*)

JUDY: Fickle! You always were stage-struck. I'm going! (*She thrusts the baby into Punch's arms, exits.*)

PUNCH: Such a beautiful baby! Just like me! (*Rocks the baby, sings, "Rock-a-bye, Baby, on the Tree Top."*)

> *Baby cries, Punch slaps it, continues:*

> Rock-a-bye, baby,
> Sleep while you can;
> If you live till you're older,
> You'll grow up a man.

Oh, you little duck! What a good, good, good baby you are!

BABY: Waaaaaaaaaaaaaa!

PUNCH: (*Knocking Baby's head against side of stage*) Go to sleep, go to sleep! (*Sings some more, desperately.*)

BABY: Waaaaaaaaaaa!

PUNCH: (*Banging harder*) Rock-a-bye, Baby, rock-a-bye, Baby!

BABY: Waaaaaaaaaaaa!

PUNCH: Bless him, he's got his father's nose. Bless me, he's got it in his teeth! Help! Murder! There, go to your mother then! (*Throws Baby offstage, calls.*) Judy, my dear, Judy!

> She's a beaut,
> But if you're going to squeeze her,
> Watch out for that enormous beezer.

Enter Judy.

JUDY: Where's the baby?

PUNCH: The baby?

JUDY: Yes, the baby.

PUNCH: What, didn't you catch him?

JUDY: Catch him?

PUNCH: Yes; I threw him out the window. I thought you might be passing.

JUDY: Oh, my poor child!

PUNCH: See here now, he was as much mine as yours.

JUDY: You beast, you cruel monster!

PUNCH: Root-ity-toot! (*They fight. Punch ducks down, comes up with club, hits the dodging Judy on the head and kills her. He lays the body out neatly across the front of the stage.*) Isn't she a beauty! (*Dances, sings.*)

> She's as blue,
> As a peacock's tail,
> She's as dead,
> As an old doornail.

Pat the Policeman enters.

PAT: All right, all right, I am here.

PUNCH: All right, all right, so am I! (*Whacks Pat on the head with the club.*)

PAT: See here now, I'll have no more of that!

PUNCH: Oh, do have another. (*Whacks him again. They fight, pause face to face.*)

PAT: Take your nose away from my face, sir!

PUNCH: Take your face away from my nose, sir!

PAT: You have committed an aggravated assault and contempt of court, sir, and I am under the painful necessity of taking you in.

PUNCH: And I am under the painful necessity of knocking you out! (*Kills Pat with a blow of his club, lays the body out beside the other, counts them gloatingly.*) One, two, doodle-dee-doo, not a bad day's work.

Enter Toby the dog.

PUNCH: Ah, my dog, Toby, man's best friend! Dear Toby, nice Toby, good Toby. (*Pats Toby, embraces him, becomes soppily sentimental, weeping to the dog.*) Oh, Toby, if you only knew. I am surrounded by enemies. See them there, one, two, doodle-ee-doo. Nobody loves old Punch. Old Punch has nobody in the world, nobody but you, dear Toby. (*Pauses, peers angrily at Toby.*) Well, what have you got to say to that? (*Toby seizes his nose in his teeth.*) Help! Murder! Traitorized! (*Toby hangs on; they lurch from one side of the stage to the other. Punch manages to get hold of his club, gives the dog a tremendous clout.*

Toby collapses; Punch hops about holding his nose.) Oh, ouch, my nose, my dear nose, man's best friend! (*Notices dead dog, lines the body up with the other two.*) Still, it was worth it. (*Dances, sings.*) One, two, *three,* doodle-doodle-*dee!*

Enter Scaramouche.

SCARAMOUCHE: See here, Mr. Punch, I'm returning this letter. You forgot to put a stamp on it.

PUNCH: Did I now? (*Whacks him on head.*) There, how's that?

SCARAMOUCHE: But this letter is special delivery!

PUNCH: Oh, is it? Sorry. (*Whacks him on backside.*)

SCARAMOUCHE: Now, now, you can't fool me, Mr. Punch. You have to pay certain amounts of money for certain letters. I know. I have it all here in my head.

PUNCH: Where is that?

SCARAMOUCHE: (*obligingly bends head forward.*) Here, in my head.

PUNCH: Ah! Well, I think I'll send that air mail. (*Strikes head with club and sends it sailing. Scaramouche runs around headless, finally topples over on the edge of the stage. Punch lines the body up neatly with the rest, singing.*) One, two, three, *four,* every moment brings one more. Root-ity-toot-ity-toot!

Enter Jack Ketch the Hangman.

J. KETCH: Mr. Punch, you are my prisoner.

PUNCH: What for?

J. KETCH: For having broken the laws of the land.

PUNCH: But I never touched them.

J. KETCH: Anyhow, you are to be hanged.

PUNCH: Hanged! Oh dear!

J. KETCH: Yes, and I hope it will be a lesson to you. (*Sticks gallows into bracket on back edge of playboard.*)

PUNCH: But what about my poor wife and sixteen small children, most of them twins and the oldest only three years of age!

J. KETCH: Mr. Punch, you are to be hanged by the neck till you are dead, dead, dead!

PUNCH: What! Three times?

J. KETCH: I expect once will be enough. Put your head in this noose.

PUNCH: (*Pretending to thrust his head into noose, missing completely.*) Where? There?

J. KETCH: No, no, a little further to the right.

PUNCH: I'm not very good at this. I was never hanged before, you know. Here? No, there. Oops, missed again.

J. KETCH: No, no, you've got it all wrong. I suppose I'll have to show you how. Now then, keep an eye on me. I take aim, put my head slowly forward and thrust it into the noose, so! (*Puts his head in the noose.*)

PUNCH: Ah, now I see! (*Pulls rope tight, hanging the hang-man.*) Yes, indeedle-ee-dee, I see! Root-ity-toot! Here's a man hung up to dry! (*Lays the body out with the rest.*) One, two, three, four, *five;* and nary a man is left alive! Hurrah, hurrah!

Ghost rises behind him.

GHOST: Boo-o-o-oh!

PUNCH: (*Terrified*) Help, help!

GHOST: You are wanted.

PUNCH: But where and what for?

GHOST: In the other world, to answer for your misdeeds.

PUNCH: Wait a minute. Whom were you to ask for?

GHOST: For the man who was to be hanged.

PUNCH: Oh, the man who was to be hanged. Well, that's him there, obviously. (*Points to body of hangman.*)

GHOST: Oh, I beg your pardon. (*Bends over hangman.*)

PUNCH: (*Raising his club.*) Let me beg yours. (*Kills ghost with one blow.*) I can hardly believe it! Surely this must be a record bag! One, two, three, four, five, *six;* there they lie, the silly sticks! (*He dances, sings.*) Root-ity-toot-ity-toot! (*Dancing back and forth across the stage, he returns from the wings a last time to discover The Devil dancing with him, matching him step for step.*)

PUNCH: What's this? There seems to be one I've missed.

DEVIL: (*Looking him over.*) I beg your pardon, there seems to be one *I've* missed.

PUNCH: See here now, who are you?

DEVIL: You can call me Nick.

PUNCH: The devil you say!

DEVIL: You've got it right the first time. I think you've met your match, Mr. Punch. (*He aims his pitchfork.*) I want *you!*

PUNCH: But — — — but I don't want you! (*The Devil lunges; Punch is forced to defend himself. A furious battle rages, but his club is no match for the pitchfork. The fatal thrust goes home; Punch crumples slowly down, beseeching.*) Oh, oh, I am dying. Pray for me, children, I was such a good man. One, two, three, four, five, six—seven. (*He falls into place at the bottom of the row.*) (*The Devil hoists him on his pitchfork.*)

DEVIL: Root-ity-too! Serves him right,
Wicked Mr. Punch has been put to flight;
Ladies and gentlemen all, good night,
To the freaks of Punch and Judy!

The Devil carries Punch off to Purgatory.

Curtain.

(*Final note: in an older English version, Punch wins the battle with the Devil and hoists him on his own pitchfork, crying triumphantly, "Hurrah, hurrah! The Devil is dead; now we can all do as we like!"*)

47. DUSTY RODENT

The head for this cheery little chipmunk is made from
cast plastic wood, which can be purchased by the can or
tube. But before the finished head can be cast, a plasticine
model must be made and a plaster mould made from it.

Making a Split Plaster Mould

Model your plasticine head, then cut it in two halves by
drawing a strong thread or thin wire down through it as
shown in the illustration, A. This is not as easy as it looks
and should be done slowly and carefully. It is easier with
someone else holding the head in the palms of his hands
with the features up and the neck pointed toward the cutter,
as shown, B. The two halves of the head are then placed
with their flat sides down in a frame about three inches
deep. Mix plaster of Paris into about 2 pints of water, *adding the plaster to the water,* until it is the consistency of

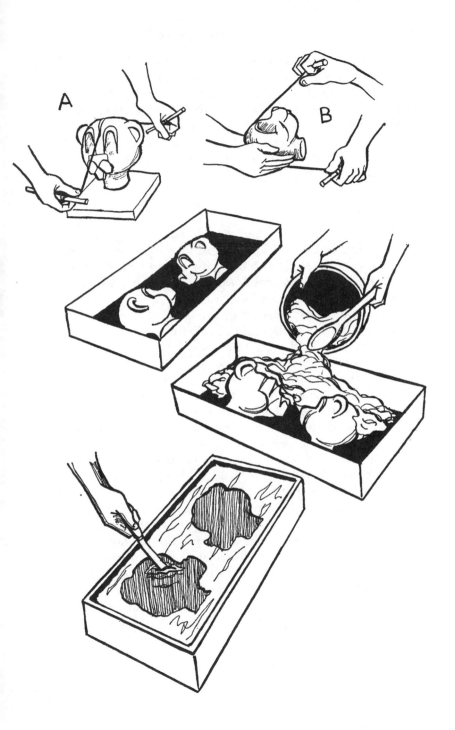

thick cream. Pour this slowly over the two halves of the head, making sure there are no bubbles against the plasticine. Fill the frame until the highest parts of the plasticine halves are covered by at least ½ inch of plaster. When the mould is dry, turn it over and remove the halves by carefully prying them out with a screw driver. Break off any overhang of plaster around the edges of the two depressions, and your mould is ready.

Casting Plastic Wood

The inside surface of the mould must be lightly but thoroughly greased with Vaseline before the plastic wood is applied. Fingers should also be lightly coated with Vaseline for handling the plastic wood. Apply it carefully, pressing it firmly into all the features of the mould, A, and trying to maintain a uniform thickness of an eighth of an inch. The wood must be left to dry naturally. Do not use direct artificial heat. Test the dryness of the wood by pressing at the thickest part; it should be rock hard. Remove the two halves of the head from the mould by lifting from the back edges, B. Join the two halves together as soon as possible, as they tend to warp if left standing. If the edges do not butt together evenly, you can trim them with a sharp knife or by rubbing them gently in a circular motion on a piece of sandpaper lying flat on a table. Trim the bottom edges of the neck on each half so that they match. Prepare the edges for joining by first putting glue around the edges of both halves. Then put a little plastic wood on top of the glue all around the edge *of one side only*. Place the halves together, lining up the features at the front of the head carefully, C. The back can be fixed later. Build a small rim around the bottom of the neck, D, to aid in joining the head to the body later. Smooth the excess wood and glue into the joint and allow to dry. The head can be finished with added plastic wood and careful sanding.

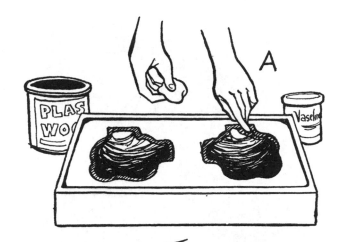

A

B

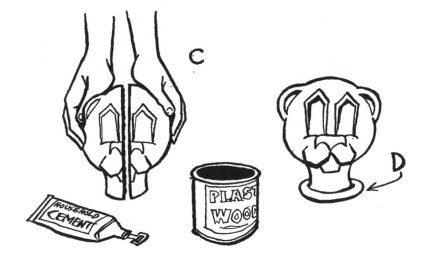

C

D

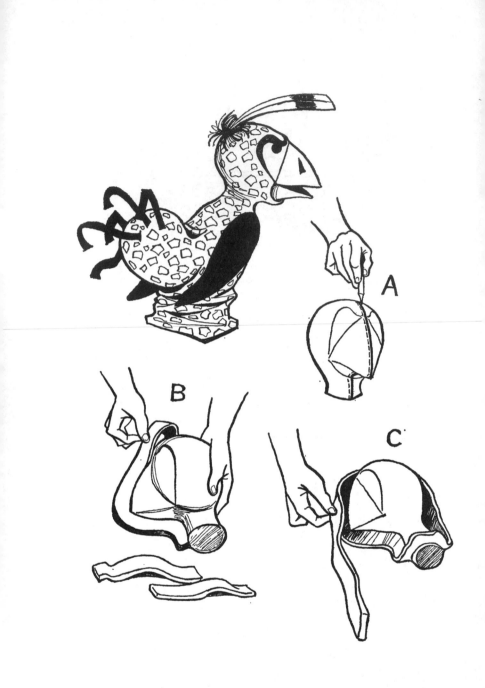

A

B

C

48. BIRD McDERMITT

This sour-faced bird has a movable beak with which he pronounces his prophecies of doom. His body can be made out of any old speckled rag and bit of feather lying around the house. His head can be cast in plastic wood or in papier-mâché. The overcasting in papier-mâché explained earlier results in a loss of some detail, as the paper is built up over the model. But by casting the papier-mâché *inside* a mould, as with plastic wood, you can retain most detail. However, papier-mâché has to be cast in a more complicated mould—a shim cast mould.

Making a Shim Cast Mould

Shims are anything which divide; in this case, strips of plasticine. Divide your plasticine model head by drawing a faint line running through the center of the features and down the center of the back of the head as in A. Prepare strips of plasticine about ¾ inch wide and ⅛ inch thick. Apply these strips along the line you have drawn so that there is a small, upright wall of plasticine running all the way around the head like a crest, as in B. Now lay the head on its side in a nest of soft paper. Take another long strip of plasticine and run it around the dividing crest so that it forms a sealed trough, C, that will contain the plaster. The neck of the plasticine model should stick out free of this trough at the bottom. Now heap plaster into the trough, making sure it fills in against all the features. Build up the plaster so that it covers the entire side of the head, D, then smooth it off a little on top so that when it dries and is turned over, it will sit flat. When the plaster is dry, turn the mould over and remove the plasticine dividers to expose the ¾-inch plaster shelf or margin, E. With a pointed knife, scrape this shelf until it is flat and smooth, then into it dig three holes, F,

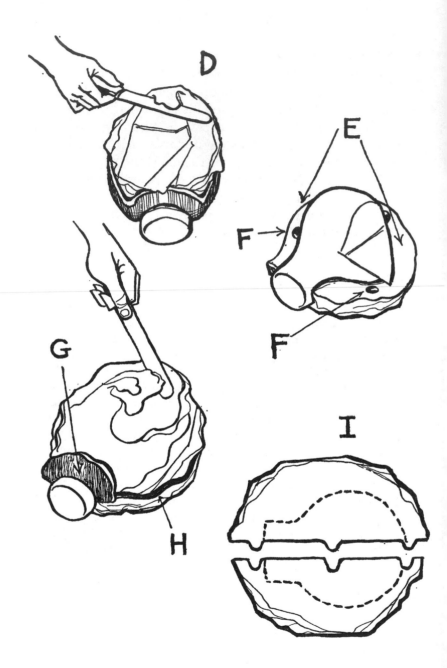

about ½ inch deep: one opposite the chin, one over the top of the head, one opposite the back of the neck—all in the center of the margin's width. These holes will line up with lugs and keep the two halves of the mould in line when the other half is poured. Put a little collar of plasticine around the bottom of the neck, G, so that the neck again thrusts free. Grease the surface of the margin or shelf thoroughly, making sure to get a good coating down into the lug holes.

Now pour plaster over the head and scrape it clean where it runs over the edge of the shelf so that the dividing crack between the first and second halves of the mould is clearly visible, H. Pack the plaster up over the head, covering it completely. When it is dry, tap the mould gently in a number of places around the crack and pry the two halves gently apart. Remove the plasticine. Fill any inside bubble holes with plaster, smoothing the patch with your finger. The two halves should fit snugly together, I, the lugs of the one half fitting neatly into the lug holes of the other, the only opening being where the neck of the model thrusts out.

You now have a cast that can be used for casting papier-mâché, celastic, latex or plaster. It can be used again and again, if you take care of it. Store your casts carefully in boxes with shaving or paper excelsior cushions. Many puppeteers use the same mould for a number of characters, counting on painting and dressing to add the required character differences.

Casting Papier-Mâché

Shellac both halves of the shim cast mould and allow it
to dry well. This time you might add half a teaspoon of alum
to the cold water papier-mâché paste for added strength,
mixing it in thoroughly. In addition to the strips of newspaper, you might use strips of finer paper, such as that used
in Japanese crepe napkins. This is not absolutely necessary,
but will give your heads a finer outside finish. Do not grease
the mould. Pass the strips of finer paper quickly through
clean water, then paste them lightly *on one side only* and
press them into the mould with the *pasted side up*. Make
sure the paper lies perfectly flat without creases or bubbles
and that the inside surface of the mould is covered completely.

Allow the paper to overlap the top edge of the mould
about 1 inch all the way around, as in A. Give the first coat
of paper a thin coat of paste. Add another complete layer
of the thinner paper exactly as you did the first. Make sure
it is thoroughly pressed into the features to get full defini-
tion from the mould. Now draw the strips of newspaper
through the paste mixture and begin to lay down your third
coat. This time omit the 1-inch overlap over the top edge
of the mould. Add two or three more complete layers of
newspaper. Now paper the second half of the mould as you
did the first, but allow *all coats of both grades of paper*
to overlap the top edge of the mould. When this half is prepared, turn the overlap inward from the top edge, B, but do
not allow it to droop down into the mould. You might have
to shorten it by tearing, but keep it as wide as possible, for
it is going to secure the inside of your seam. Now lower this
half of the mould over the first one, lining the lugs and lug
holes up, C. Holding the two halves tightly together, run
your finger around the inside of the neck, smoothing the
overlap down across the seam inside. Work as far as you

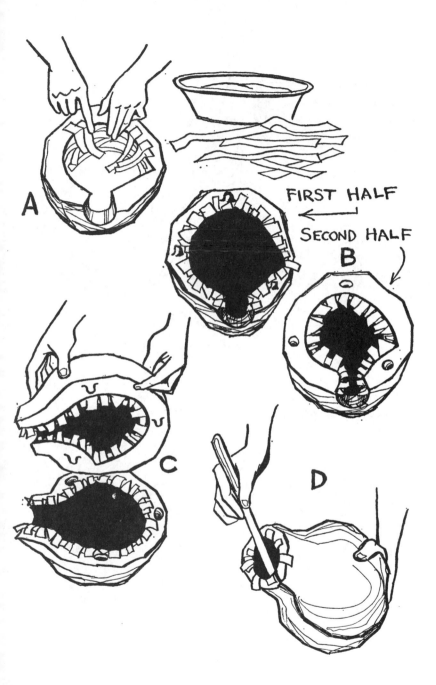

A

FIRST HALF

SECOND HALF

B

C

D

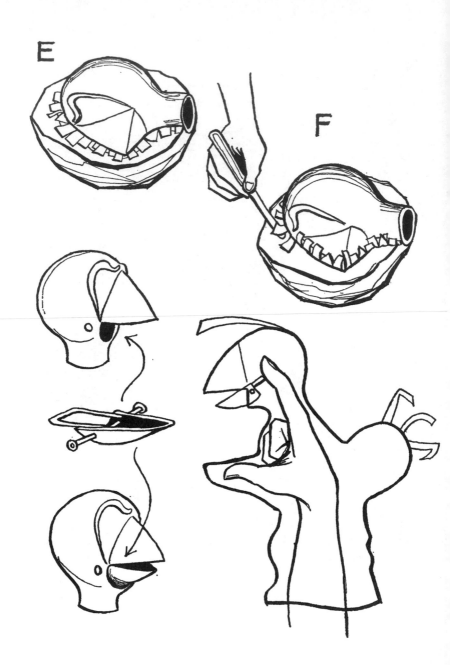

E

F

can up into the head, sealing the overlap over the seam. The overlap which you cannot reach can be smoothed with a stick pushed up into the neck, as in D. Add a reinforcing collar of paste-soaked newspaper around the inside of the neck. Now carefully remove this half of the plaster mould, jiggling gently in case any paste has soaked through the first layers and stuck to the plaster. The overlap of lighter paper from the first half of the mould will be revealed, F, lying flat on the shelf or margin. Shorten this overlap to about ¼ inch, then with the edge of a knife lift it up and press it carefully onto the paper head, thus securing the outside of the seam, as in E and F. A thin coat of paste will flatten it smoothly against the head. Allow the exposed half of the head to dry until it holds shape. Remove the head from the mould and rest it on the drier side and allow it to dry thoroughly all over. To further strengthen it, you can paint it with a final thin coat of paste.

Making a Movable Mouth

To make Bird's movable beak, overcast a papier-mâché lower jaw, cut a hole in the head to receive it and rig it as shown. The beak is controlled with the tip of the finger inside the puppet's head. A good deal of experimentation and practice will be necessary before you will discover the proper rigging to fit your hand and perfect the method of moving the mouth, but in the end, you'll have a talking bird!

49. KLONDIKE KITTY

This feline vamp has long-lashed eyes, a tight-fitting sheath dress of mustard velvet, and a long white furry tail which she drapes up over her shoulders like an ermine stole. Her head can be cast in plastic wood, papier-mâché or Celastic.

Casting Celastic

Celastic is the trade name of a material that makes light, practically unbreakable puppet heads. It is expensive compared to plastic wood or papier-mâché. The material is purchased by the yard along with some acetone and a special parting agent which prevents it from sticking to the plaster mould. The mould should be wetted, then the parting agent brushed on. The Celastic is torn in strips and made pliable with the acetone. It is then laid in the mould much the same as in casting papier-mâché, although two layers are usually enough. Always work in a well-ventilated room and use rubber gloves to protect your hands.

Movable Eyes

Movable eyes should be mounted in the front half of the head before the two halves are joined together. They can be made of wooden beads or doll eyes. Kitty's eyelashes are of the kind purchased at cosmetic counters. Her eyes are controlled by the tip of the finger inside the puppet head, but movable eyes can also be operated by a wire passed down through the body. This method occupies both the operator's hands, however.

50. FLAK J. FROG

The bug-eyed gentleman in the camel's-hair coat with the carnation in his buttonhole is a super-drummer, an advertising man. His hands are permanently fixed to his stomach because the operator's whole hand is up inside his head. His smile is flexible and liquid because his head is made of rubber, or to be more exact, latex.

Casting Latex

There are several commercial latex mixtures that dry without oven curing. Pliatex is one of them, sold by Sculpture House in New York City. No separating solution is needed with Pliatex. The casting rubber is mixed with a special casting filler, the proportions depending on the amount of flexibility desired. Flak J. Frog was cast from a mixture of three parts rubber to one part filler. The filler should always be *added to* the rubber. The mixture is poured into a shim cast plaster mould and allowed to "build up" to desired thickness, usually from 15 to 30 minutes. The excess liquid is then poured out and the mould is allowed to drain for 10 minutes or more. It is then removed and allowed to air dry or is dried in an oven at 150 to 180 degrees. Flexible latex casts can be decorated only with special latex paints, available wherever latex is sold. You can make a rubber patching compound by mixing casein glue with Pliatex filler.

51. TALKING STORYBOOK

His face is a flexible latex mask fixed to the front of a false book. There is a hole at the back, through which the operator reaches, fitting his hand into the nose and lower jaw to open and shut the mouth.

the
OLD YARN SPINNER

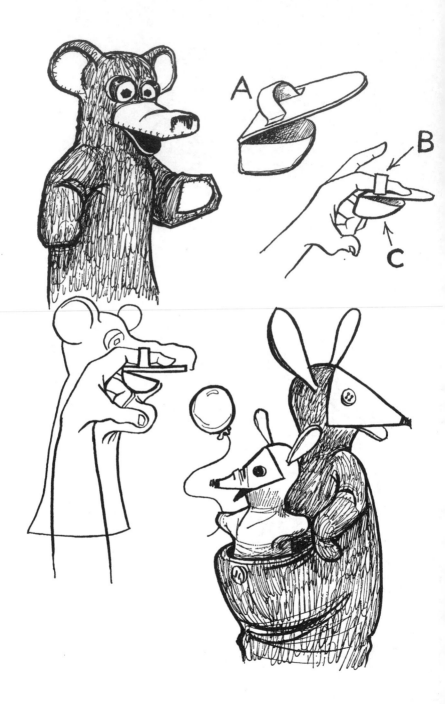

A

B

C

52. YANKEE PANKY

Yankee Panky, the All-American bear, is made of cardboard, felt and an old overcoat. His body is cut from a woman's overcoat made of dark blue wool material with a thick nap. One great advantage of animal puppets is that they do not need to have hands. The fingers of the operator come right to the snub end of the paw and enable him to have sure and direct control over any props handled. Yankee's paws are of white felt, as is his nose. His ears are lined with white felt, his mouth with pink, and his tongue is a double thickness of red felt. His eyes are made of cardboard discs and clear discs of celluloid from a toothpaste box, glued together with a chip of black plastic sliding around inside. His mouth is moved by the puppeteer's finger, crooked inside the head and extending into the nose.

Making Cloth Animal Heads

To articulate the mouth of a cloth head, first build the skeleton construction, A, of cardboard, gluing or securing it together with strong masking tape. The operator's bent finger fits into the loop, B, raising and lowering the upper jaw against the little platform of the lower jaw, C, which rests against the folded second and third fingers. The head is then cut and sewed to fit around this construction, with the necessary cotton padding added up inside the head to give it form. Cloth is especially good for the heads of animals and fantasy characters, not so good for puppets meant to represent realistic people.

53. MIZ ROO

Mama Kangaroo is constructed just as the bear was, but of brown cloth, with bent paws and a button up pouch for:

54. WALLY ROO

Her son, who is a miniature version of his mother, is as small as the operator's hand will allow.

55. THE GREAT APE HONK KONG

Honk is an elaborate combination of overcast papier-mâché and cloth. His mouth is articulated with the full hand inside his head, and so his arms are stationary.

Cloth and Papier-Mâché Combined

Overcast papier-mâché parts are used where rigidity or a smooth texture is needed: in Honk's case, the crown of his head and his glowering brow, A, and his chest and belly, B. Cloth is then cut, sewed and glued to the papier-mâché parts to complete the puppet. A good deal of fitting and re-cutting is usually involved, so it is a good idea to have plenty of the type of cloth you plan to use. When the puppet is assembled, the exposed papier-mâché parts are painted. Honk's face, ears and belly are left exposed and painted black because these are exactly the parts of a gorilla that are hairless and shiny black. The rest of him is made of a hairy gray wool material like a gorilla's coarse coat. The upper and lower jaws are made of strong but flexible cardboard so as to make his grimaces as expressive as possible. His muzzle is made of a double layer of light gray felt. The inside of his mouth is lined with pink, his tongue is a deep scarlet, his tusks are of white felt.

56. FABIAN THE FOX

Here a rigid skull of papier-mâché was overlaid with cloth, leaving some parts exposed to be painted. The cloth used is a fur-like cotton cloth available at stores which sell display materials and where many special materials for puppets and props can be found.

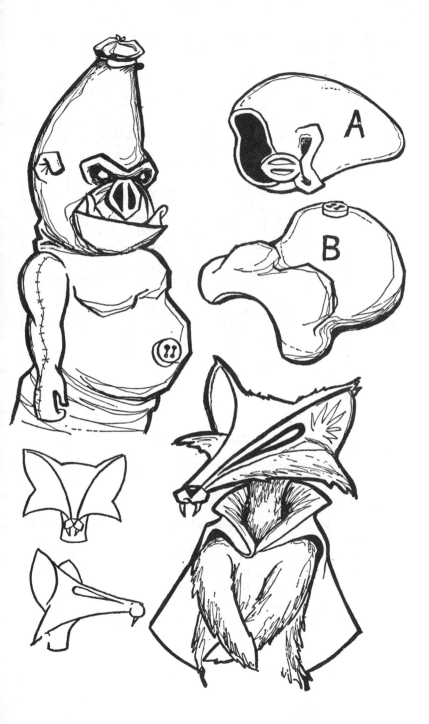

A *Permanent Professional Stage*

This stage is designed for professional performances in a more or less permanent place. It is for presentation of the type in which the operators hold the puppets overhead so it can be long and deep with plenty of room for the puppets to move about. Enough room is allowed on either side of the opening for satisfactory entrances and exits. There should be room behind for three operators to work comfortably.

Backgrounds can be painted on cloth or cardboard covered frames or on window shades, which can be fixed in series overhead and raised and lowered as needed. Lighting can be as elaborate as wished, although the strongest key lighting should come from straight out in front to prevent the puppet's eyes from being deeply shadowed. Puppets can be hung from hooks or strong spring clips behind the stage—head down so that the operators can easily thrust their hands into them and pull them free for action.

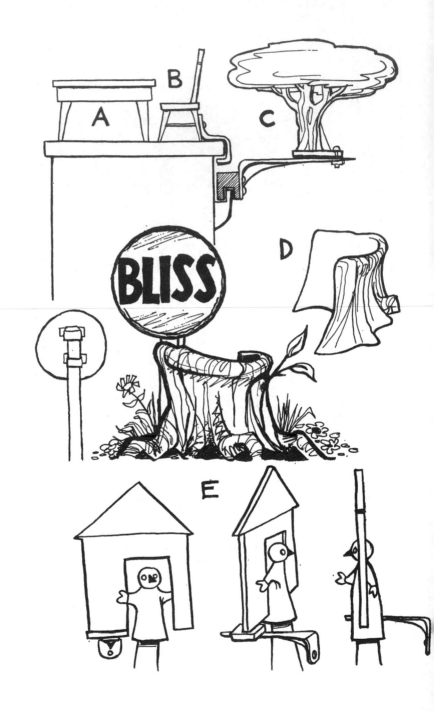

Properties

Although props can often be found in the dime store, many have to be especially made for the puppet stage. They can be placed on the playing board, as shown, A; they can be clipped to the back edge of the playing board or placed on it, as shown, B; or they can be placed further back into the playing area by use of brackets, as shown, C. Getting a puppet in and out of the doorway of a three-dimensional house is solved by use of brackets, as illustrated, E. Stairs must be shown in silhouette, of course. Paper foliage and manufactured paper ironwork and other decorations can be found in display stores. Props and set pieces that are going to be placed on brackets should be as light as possible.

Setting for a Modern Fable

Following is a play in which you can use some of the professional puppets you have made. You do not have to have all the puppets listed for the play; other puppets of suitable character can be substituted. The construction of the stump for the play is shown opposite, D. It is made in relief from quick papier-mâché, with the back open so that the puppets can appear to go in and out through the opening at the top. The round billboard should be mounted on a bracket sticking out from the side of the stage, so that the puppets can move between it and the stump, which is further forward.

THE BEAR, THE BOMB, AND THE BILLBOARD

THE BEAR, THE BOMB,
AND THE BILLBOARD

A Modern Fable in One Act

Characters:

Yankee Panky	full of fun and fancy free
Dusty Rodent	fussy and forever proper
Flak J. Frog	a drummer
Bird McDermitt	prophet of gloom, doom, and dark days ahead
Fabian Fox	vile and villainous, a scamp

Scene: A quiet glade in an evergreen forest. Center stage a hollow stump, open at the top. Directly behind the stump, a round red billboard with one word in black: BLISS!

Scene 1. *Curtain opens.*
The stage is empty. Morning birds are twittering. A great deal of groaning and yawning is heard—the sounds of someone waking up. Finally Yankee Panky appears at the top of the stump,

*rests his paws on the top edge and gazes sleepily around. He
does not notice the billboard behind him.*

YANK: A D-double dandy day! By my buttons, a D-double
dandy day indeed! Good morning, sun! Good morning,
birds! Good morning, forest! Why, it's a most unusual day.
I believe this calls for a nap. (*He starts to disappear back
into stump.*)

Dusty Rodent enters with broom, sweeping furiously.

DUSTY: Hold on there, Springcleaningtime, Springcleaningtime!

YANK (*aside*): Oh oh, here comes the grim sweeper.

DUSTY: Come on, Yank, up and at 'em. Springcleaningtime!

YANK: Spring cleaning! But Dusty, it's September.

DUSTY: A stitch in time saves nine. The early bird gets the
worm. Can't get started too soon on these things. (*He
sweeps the playboard, raising dust.*)

YANK: Why? (*Cough, cough!*) Why are you always sweeping
the forest floor!

DUSTY: It's so messy. Twigs and leaves and stones lying around.

YANK: But they lie where they fall. It's *meant* to be that way.

DUSTY: Oh no, these things have to be rearranged, tidied up.
That's our mission in life, Yank.

YANK: How can you say that! On a beautiful morning like this,

when Mother Nature has arranged things so perfectly—
(*He turns to survey forest, starts at sight of billboard, turns
back to front, stiff with shock.*) What—what is that?

DUSTY: What is what?

YANK: There behind me. What is it?

DUSTY: Oh that. That's a billboard. (*He sweeps his way offstage.*)

YANK: (*Stunned.*) A billboard. In my backyard. (*He sneaks
another look behind him, gasps and sinks down into
stump. Slowly he reappears, gasps, retreats again.*)

Enter Flak J. Frog.

FLAK: Is it still there? (*Surveys billboard proudly.*) Oh yes.
Superb! Marvelous! A gem! a MASTER-piece!

YANK: (*Reappearing*) Flak J. Frog, does that belong to you?

FLAK: To me? Well, yes, I did have a modest part in its
creation. But now it belongs to the world, to the great
commonwealth of peoples, to EVerybody!

YANK: Not to me. I don't want it. Get it out of here.

FLAK: But my friend, you've *got* it. We steamrolled it through
the forest council, leased the land and put it up. Isn't it
outstanding?

YANK: It stands out all right. What does it mean?

FLAK: Bliss? You know what that means: contentment, peace, happiness complete!

YANK: You mean they have that in the stores now?

FLAK: Well, not exactly. You see, it's a pill.

YANK: A pill?

FLAK: That's right. One-a-day Bliss Pills. One a day keeps the BLUES away. You should try some, Yank, you're looking a bit ragged this morning. (*He exits, whistling cheerily.*)

YANK: (*Shouting after him.*) I felt fine until a few minutes ago. (*Grumbling.*) It's a fiendish system. The billboards make you so nervous, you *have* to take pills. Well, I can see the time has come for me to hibernate. (*With a disgusted glance at the billboard.*) I think I'll make this one a good *long* hibernation. Let's see, everything ready down there. A year's supply of peanut butter, clean sheets—

Enter Bird McDermitt.

BIRD: Oh woe! Oh woe! I have received dark news, dark news.

YANK: (*Not glad to see him.*) Don't tell me, I don't want to hear it.

BIRD: Dark clouds, ominous shadows in my crystal ball.

YANK: You should get a new crystal ball.

BIRD: Don't mock me, Yank, I see all.

YANK: And tell all.

BIRD: Dark news, Yank. The world is to end Thursday, next, if not sooner.

YANK: How is it going to end this time?

BIRD: The bomb, Yank, the bomb! I see it in my mind's eye, the bomb! It is about to go off. I see it. I hear it, ticking, ticking—

> (*There is indeed the sound of ticking produced by rapping a stick sharply and rhythmically backstage.*)

YANK: Yikes, I hear it too!

BIRD: Yes, yes, the bomb! Ticking, ticking!

YANK: Wait a minute, that's only my alarm clock. (*He climbs down from stump, pulls clock from behind bush, climbs back up into stump with it.*) I'm going into hibernation this morning. I think I'll be down all winter this trip.

BIRD: But what do you need an alarm clock for?

YANK: I set it to wake me up every half hour to take a little peanut butter and bread. After all, one can't sleep *all* the time.

BIRD: Every half hour—

YANK: Every hour on Sunday, the day of rest.

BIRD: Are you blind? How can you sleep with the bomb ready to go off any moment. Ticking, ticking—

YANK: I beg your pardon, that's my alarm clock.

BIRD: Irresponsible indifference. For shame. I tell you, beware! Beware the bomb! (*He goes off, muttering gloomily.*)

YANK: What a morning. First the billboard, now the bomb. I'll probably have nightmares about bombs. Better take a little bread and peanut butter before retiring, that way I might dream some beautiful dream—all about bread and peanut butter. Well, to bed. (*Holding his clock, he sinks down into stump. The ticking subsides, the birds twitter.*)

Enter Fabian the Fox, stealthily, carrying a black box marked BOMB.

FABIAN: Ah, this must be the place. Yes indeed, a hollow stump, they told me, where there lives a silly bear entirely surrounded by jars of peanut butter. (*Cautiously he peers down into the stump.*) Black as pitch down there. Hmmm, perhaps he's hibernating. Well, this will bring him out. (*He places the box beside the stump.*) Nothing like a bear for curiosity. And besides, my good gloomy friend, Bird McDermitt, has planted the idea in his head. Perhaps he is dreaming of bombs even now. Peanut butter, peanut butter! Oh my, how I love peanut butter! Now to wind my clock. (*He takes an alarm clock from the box, winds it, replaces it and closes the box. The ticking begins again.*) Now to coax him from his slumber. (*He bends over the top of the stump and whispers loudly.*) Bomb, bomb, beware the bomb! Beware, bear, beware the bomb, bomb! (*He pauses. Silence.*) Hmm, sleeps like a log. (*He shouts.*) Egad, I do believe there is a BOMB up here!

There is a startled snorting from below. The stump shudders. Yank appears, wild-eyed.

YANK: Bomb, bomb! Where? Where?

FABIAN: Here, in this box clearly marked BOMB. Quickly, before it goes off, we must smother it.

YANK: But how? How?

FABIAN: With peanut butter, of course. That's the only way to smother a bomb, with peanut butter, lots of peanut butter. (*He pauses, sidles closer.*) You, uh, don't happen to have any peanut butter around, do you?

YANK: (*Waking up now, suspicious.*) Yes, I think I might have a bit tucked away in the pantry.

FABIAN: Then get it, quickly, all you have! Hurry, there's no time to think it over, Bear!

YANK: (*Knowingly*) Oh, I've had time to think it over. Very well, Fox. (*He ducks down into stump, comes up with pot marked PEANUT BUTTER. He hands this to Fabian, who pours its contents into the black box. The ticking continues.*)

FABIAN: It's still ticking! More, we must have more. More peanut butter!

> *Yank continues to bring peanut butter jars up. Fabian pours them into the box, urging him on. The ticking continues. Six or seven jars have been emptied, and Yank collapses on the rim of the stump, pretending exhaustion.*

YANK: I can't go on. Up and down this ladder. I'm tired.

FABIAN: But the bomb is still ticking!

YANK: Isn't it out yet? Well, then, let it go off. I'm too tired to go down there again.

FABIAN: But you can't give up. You'll be blown to bits. I won't let you commit suicide like this. Here, let me go down.

YANK: Very well then, if you insist. (*He steps aside. Fabian goes down into stump.*)

FABIAN: (*His voice rising faintly.*) It's so dark down—Oof! Stumbled! Which way do I go?

YANK: Further back. Keep going. The peanut butter is there. You'll find it— (*He continues to encourage the Fox while turning to the billboard and pulling it off its stand.*)

YANK: (*to himself*) I knew I'd find a use for this thing.

FABIAN: (*voice sounding fainter*) But there's no peanut butter here, only an empty shelf—

YANK: (*Holding the billboard over the opening in the stump.*) On the table. In the spoon. There must be a good mouthful there.

FABIAN: A mouthful! I've been tricked! Let me out—what . . . what's that ticking down here? It's so dark. I can't see. What *is* that ticking!

YANK: Well now, it *could* be a bomb.

FABIAN: A bomb! Oh no! No! Let me out!

YANK: Later, Mr. Fox. (*He jambs the billboard down tight, lidding the stump securely. The ticking stops. He turns to the box marked BOMB, chuckling to himself.*) Poor fellow has bombs on the brain. He needs a rest, a long rest—say, until Spring.

  Enter Dusty, sweeping.

DUSTY: Fallcleaningtime, fallcleaningtime!

YANK: What happened to springcleaningtime?

DUSTY: Oh, that's all done. Never an idle moment. By next year I should be a year ahead. (*Yank starts out with the box.*) Hey, where are you going?

YANK: To hibernate.

DUSTY: Without your alarm clock? Without your peanut butter?

YANK: I have both in this box. The alarm clock belongs to Mr. Fox, but it'll do.

DUSTY: But where's your alarm clock?

YANK: (*Pointing to sealed stump.*) Down in the stump with Mr. Fox.

DUSTY: But what's he doing down there?

YANK: He's hibernating too, I expect. Well, toodle-oo, happy fall cleaning. (*He wanders off, humming cheerily.*)

DUSTY: (*With a puzzled look at stump.*) Hmmn, I didn't know foxes hibernated. And the billboard is gone too. Strange morning. Well, to work, I've a whole forest to tidy up. (*He sweeps his way out. The ticking resumes faintly, comes up strongly. The fox's voice is heard calling feebly.*)

FABIAN: The bomb, the bomb, help, the bomb!

The ticking subsides slowly. The birds twitter.

Curtain.

Special Puppets

B RIEFLY DESCRIBED here are three unusual types of hand puppet: finger puppets, rod puppets and shadow puppets. The little finger puppets can do little else but walk and dance, but they do that very well. Rod puppets can be used most effectively for serious narrative presentations such as Biblical Tableaus. Shadow puppets are also best suited to formal, tableau-like presentations.

57. PIROUETTE

Her body (there is only the torso and the head) can be overcast in papier-mâché, cast in plastic wood or made by bending double a piece of foam rubber, binding it with adhesive tape and adding pipe cleaner arms as in A. The torso is held in place on the first and second fingers by two loops of elastic attached to the waist as shown, B. Your fingers are the legs. Make her silver dancing slippers of foil and her arms of pipe cleaners or cloth and add cloth or paper hands. Mask your wrist with black cloth and have her dance against a dark background.

58. PIETRE

This little Swiss clog dancer is made like Pirouette,

except that his legs are extended with little built-up shoes and stockings.

59. HILDA

His dancing partner has her knees bare too—your knuckles, of course. Finger puppets perform on small stages with open tops, so the operators can reach down into them with the puppets on their hands.

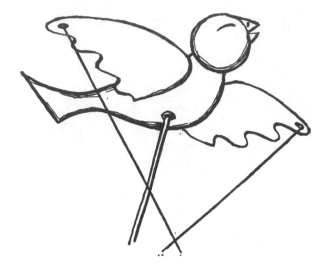

60. SUZUME-SAN THE SPARROW

The little bird's body should be cast in papier-mâché for lightness. Her wings are cut from cardboard or moulded Celastic and attached loosely to the body. They can be decorated with real feathers, as can the tail. Three stiff wires are needed for control from below: one to support the body, one to control each wing tip.

Rod Puppets

Construction can become very complicated. Figure A suggests a rod puppet with the operator's hand inside the body, the finger controlling the head, the arms controlled by rods. Figure B suggests a head on a dowel, controlled by the operator's hand inside the body. Figure C shows a fully articulated rod puppet body made of cloth and wood. The weight of the puppet is carried on a control wooden dowel running up between the legs and through the body to a point just above the shoulder yoke. The neck rests on the extension of this dowel, leaving the head free to move right

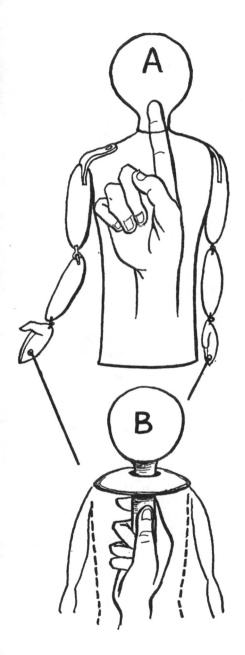

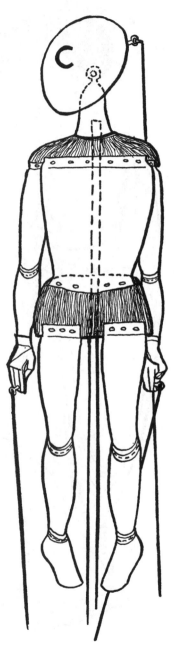

and left. The head can also be made to nod with a control wire attached at the back, as shown. The control rods on hands and feet are attached loosely to eye screws to allow free movement. They should be both light and strong and can be made from umbrella ribs or bicycle spokes for lightness and strength. This body is made of cloth stuffed with kapok and tacked to the two wooden pieces at the shoulders and hips. A good marionette book will offer further details on fully articulated bodies. Also, see No. 76.

61. SUZUME-SAN THE PRINCESS

She consists of only head, torso and delicate arms made of fine white cloth, stuffed with kapok and sewed across at elbow and wrist. Her torso is also of stuffed cloth or of wood. Her kimono drapes down from the waist, hiding the fact that she has no legs and is supported by a wooden dowel running up into her waist. She needs only two control rods, one at each wrist. With practice, one puppeteer should be able to make her move gracefully. Her head is stationary as shown. If you wish, it can be controlled by a wire as previously illustrated. Maybe you will be lucky enough to find a Chinese or Japanese doll head. If not, try to model her head after such dolls pictured in books in the library. A Japanese doll will also show you how to design her costume.

Casting Plaster

The Princess' head can be cast in fine plaster. Plaster can be finely carved and smoothed and it simulates the white complexion of a powdered Oriental maiden. A plaster head can be cast from a plaster shim cast mould. Make sure the mould is well greased and that the plaster is thoroughly mixed.

62. THE OLD MAN

This elderly Chinese peasant has movable arms, but no legs. His head can be cast or made from a dried apple (See No. 84). To get the proper stoop to his old shoulders, tilt his body on the main dowel.

63. THE OLD WOMAN

Her ragged skirts hide the fact that she, too, is without legs. Attach the spoon permanently in her hands. Attach the bowl in which she will mix her rice cakes to the top of her prop table. Her head can also be made from a dried apple—or both her and her husband's heads can be made from quick papier-mâché. In this case the irregularity and wrinkles of quick papier-mâché will be a good thing.

64. A HANDMAIDEN

She is made like the princess, but is not so pretty or so beautifully dressed. Attach her Oriental tamborine or timbrel securely to her right hand.

65. A BOX OF DEMONS

When this box is opened with a rod from below, a bunch of grinning devils leap up and dance and jiggle. One or two of them are on rods and agitate the rest, which are stuck to springs attached inside the box. Make the devils from quick papier-mâché or buy small lacquered devil masks from an Oriental gift shop. The lid of the box is held in place by a spring catch, released by a string or rod from below.

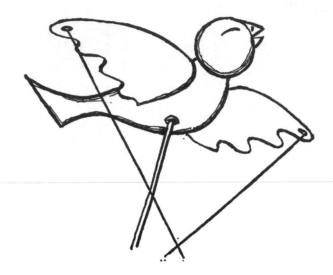

THE TONGUE-CUT
SPARROW

THE TONGUE-CUT SPARROW

A Narrated Chinese Folk Tale

1 Act, 3 Scenes

Characters:

THE NARRATOR	an offstage voice
SUZUME-SAN	the sparrow
SUZUME-SAN	the Princess
OLD MAN	the hero
OLD WOMAN	the villainess
HANDMAIDEN	the Princess' attendant

Scenes:

SCENE   I. Half exterior yard, half interior.
SCENE II. Half court, half interior of a lavish palace.
SCENE III. Same as Scene I.

A NOTE ON PRODUCTION: *Recorded or live music can be used throughout. The narrator speaks from a position in the shadows beside the stage or entirely out of sight of the audience. Puppet movement should be graceful and highly stylized. Decoration of foliage and flowers fixed to the sides of the stage does not have to be removed with scene changes. Three backgrounds should be painted as expressively but as simply as possible on window shades, the third being a duplicate of the first. These rolled shades are arranged in sequence. Scene changes take place in full view of the audience: the shades are simply rolled slowly up at the ends of fine wires as the puppet appears to move from one locale to the other. Lighting changes can help make these changes quite impressive.*

Oriental music.

NARRATOR: Once, not very long ago as time goes in Northern China, a very old woman and a very old man lived together in a tumble-down bamboo house.

The lights come up slowly. We see a barren yard on stage right of the background; the interior of a rude bamboo hut on the left. At a table in front of the interior the old woman moves her spoon wearily around in a bowl.

NARRATOR: All their lives they had lived in this miserable house; all their lives they had toiled together for very little—a bowl of rice, a bit of fish and a rice cake at the end of the day. They had no tea. They had no wine. They had no children. They had nothing but the tumble-down house and each other. And all of this endless toil for so little had made the old woman bitter.

The old woman begins to mutter to herself at her work. The sound is faint, Oriental, unintelligible. She is the only one who speaks, and her jabber is meant only as a background sound.

NARRATOR: She had become a shrew. All day as she worked she complained to herself, waiting for the old man to come in from their shabby rice paddy—waiting to complain to him.

The old man appears stage right, hobbling along painfully but briskly. He is carrying something in his hands, but we can't quite tell what it is.

NARRATOR: Usually the old man arrived silent and remained silent all through the long evening, while his wife scolded him. But this night he was talking away excitedly as he came.

Old man gestures, hobbles excitedly.

NARRATOR: "I have a gift for you," he called, "a wonderful gift!"

"A gift?" Quickly the old woman got up from her work and went to greet him, her eyes shining with greed. "A gift! What is it?"

She meets him at the door. He turns to face the audience and at the same time opens his hands.

NARRATOR: "A sparrow! A beautiful little sparrow!" cried the old man.

The sparrow flutters free of his hands, rises lamely a moment, then falls to lie fluttering on the playboard.

NARRATOR: "But she has a broken wing. We must care for her until it is mended. How do you like my gift? Isn't she pretty? Some boys must have hit her with a stone. I found her lying broken in the fields."

"And it's back to the field she goes!" cries the old woman, turning her back. "You know we can't feed a bird. Why, some days there is scarcely enough rice in the house for the two of us. Back to the fields with the bird I say!"

The old man picks the bird up tenderly and follows his wife into the house. She sits at her bowl, muttering. He tends the bird in a corner.

NARRATOR: But the old man would not take the sparrow back to the fields. All that night he tended the little bird, binding its wing, feeding it drops of water squeezed from a soft little rag. But the old woman scolded and muttered and complained, heaping abuse upon her husband, upon the sparrow, upon the gods who had given her such a miserable life.

During the preceding speech the fall of night is indicated by fading the light to near darkness. At the same time the two puppets crumple very slowly to sleeping poses. When the light comes up again, they arise as if from sleep.

NARRATOR: The first thing the old man did when he arose in the morning was to see to the sparrow. The little bird was mending well under his tender care. It hopped cheerfully about and its feathers were quite glossy.

The bird sings, a clear, beautiful warbling.

NARRATOR: "Listen!" the old man cried, "listen to the beautiful song. Do you see how grateful she is for our care!"

"For your waste of time, you fool," scoffed the old woman. "What about the fields? Have you given up working to play with birds?"

Ah, yes. The old man nodded his head wearily. With one

last tender look at his little sparrow, he hobbled away into
the fields.

> *He moves slowly off stage right, the bird's song fading
> as he disappears. The old woman sits down to her
> work, muttering. The bird is still and silent in the
> corner.*

NARRATOR: The old woman took up her discontented muttering eagerly, as some women take up their mending. The
more she complained to herself, the angrier she became.
What right had he to bring home this silly bird, when he
could barely provide enough to feed the two of them! The
soft-hearted old fool! It was a shame the boys hadn't killed
the silly bird with their stones.

> *Suddenly the bird begins to sing. The old woman
> whirls on it angrily.*

NARRATOR: "Stop it! Stop that singing, you ninny! I am no soft-
hearted fool. You can't charm me with your song!"

But the bird continued to raise its beautiful voice, as if
pleading with the old woman to love it. The old woman
flew into a rage.

> *She scuttles over to the bird and strikes it down with
> her spoon, then crouches over it with her back to the
> audience.*

NARRATOR: She bent muttering over the stricken bird. She
drew a sharp knife from her belt and bent to pry the
delicate yellow beak apart.

> *The warbling is cut off short.*

NARRATOR: "There!" she said, "without a tongue, you will sing no more, my pretty."

She throws the bird out the door and goes back to her table. The bird arises feebly and flutters along the ground and off right. The old woman works away, grumbling.

NARRATOR: The day passed into afternoon and afternoon into evening. And finally, when the sky was red with the dying sun, the old man hurried in from the fields, eager to see his little bird and to hear its beautiful song again.

The old man enters right, hurries across and into hut, looks frantically around for the bird.

NARRATOR: "But where is my sparrow, where is my little Suzume-San?" he cried.

"In the fields where she belongs," the old woman replied spitefully. "I threw her out. And you needn't be listening for her song, either. No bird can sing without a tongue!"

"Oh no! You didn't, you didn't!" cried the old man.

"Oh yes, I did! That bird will never sing again."

The sparrow's song is heard, distant, beautiful. The old woman staggers back, holding her hands to her ears. The old man hurries to the door.

NARRATOR: "No, no," cried the old woman. "I don't believe it. I won't listen!"

"I believe it!" cried the old man. "It is my Suzume-San! She is calling me to hear! I'm coming, Suzume-San, I'm coming!"

He hurries out right, leaving the old woman cowering in the corner. His pace slows as he crosses the yard, moves down to face front, hobbling slowly. The old woman sinks out of sight; the scene begins to change.

NARRATOR: So the old man hobbled out into the night, leaving his wife huddled in fear. All through the long night he traveled, following the beautiful song of the sparrow. And in the morning, just as the sun was flushing the bamboo forests with fresh new color, he found himself in a strange and beautiful place, and the song of the sparrow was very near.

The old man stands in a palace courtyard stage right. The song of the sparrow rises in intensity. The Princess Suzume-San moves slowly in from stage left, followed by her handmaiden. The song of the sparrow blends with music and fades as the music comes up. The old man turns, amazed, and stumbles forward to bow at the feet of the princess.

NARRATOR: The princess spoke, and her voice was more beautiful than that of any bird. "It is I, Suzume-San, the sparrow with the broken wing whom you saved from the fields."

The old man rises, listening in amazement to her words.

NARRATOR: "I was turned into a sparrow by the spell of a wicked witch, who declared that the spell could only be broken by an act of complete and unselfish kindness. It was your kindness, old man, that freed me."

"But—but—your tongue!" cried the old man.

The Princess laughed. "You cannot tongue-cut a sparrow

that does not exist, can you? Your shrew of a wife was taking her vengeance on empty air, as usual. Now come. Sit and eat, and I will dance for you."

And the old man sat on cushions of fine silk and brocade and ate of fresh fruits and rich puddings and drank the purest of rice wines, while the beautiful Suzume-San danced for him.

The old man sits on sumptuous cushions, and Suzume-San dances for him to beautiful music, while her handmaiden sits to the side, swaying gracefully and tapping her timbrel in time to the music.

NARRATOR: When she had danced for him, Suzume-San clapped her hands three times.

Sharp backstage claps match the movement of her hands. The handmaiden brings out a golden chest.

NARRATOR: "Take this as your reward," the princess told him. "And may the gods go with you, old man."

The music rises. The princess drifts out left. The song of the sparrow is heard, then fades. The old man lifts the box and starts out slowly right. The scene begins to change again.

NARRATOR: So the old man took up the golden chest and started home. He was another night in traveling, for the chest was heavy. And finally he arrived at his own poor house.

He finds himself in his barren yard. The old woman is at her work and her grumbling. She rises, chattering angrily.

NARRATOR: The moment she saw him, his wife began to scold. And then she saw the box. "Gold!" she cried.

"It was given to me by a princess," the old man explained. "You see, my Suzume-San was not really a sparrow at all—"

"Never mind, never mind, it's gold!" gloated the old woman. "This time you have really brought me a gift!"

"But it is my reward," faltered the old man.

"Nonsense, you old fool," she scolded. "It is *ours*. Everything is shared between us. Don't you remember the marriage vows? Now, quickly, open it up, open it up!" And without waiting for him, she impatiently rushed at the box and tore it open!

> *To a din of music the box bursts open and goggling, grinning demons pop out. The old woman staggers back in a swoon and falls in a heap to the floor. The old man closes the box and turns toward her uncertainly. At that moment the song of the sparrow is heard, and Suzume-San appears right, followed by her handmaiden. They move gracefully across the yard and into the hut.*

NARRATOR: "Suzume-San!" cried the old man. "What has happened to her, to my wife?"

"She will be all right," replied the princess with a smile. "She has only fainted."

"But the box of devils. Was it meant for me?"

"No, it was meant for her."

"But how did you know she would open it?"

"Perhaps I know your wife better than you do yourself, old man. At any rate, she did open it and she got her reward. Now here is yours."

The princess hands the old man an enormous pearl.

NARRATOR: "The largest pearl in the kingdom. Take it, and with it buy yourself a new farm and buy your wife a new house and a new dress. Perhaps she will change her ways then."

"Oh, thank you, thank you, Suzume-San," said the old man.

"Please," said the princess, "don't thank me. You did me a great kindness. The saying is more than 'one kindness deserves another.' It should be: 'One kindness deserves a greater.' Good-by, my kindly old man."

"Good-by, good-by," cried the old man, "good-by, my Suzume-San!"

The princess and her handmaiden move slowly off right. The song of the sparrow drifts back, then becomes music. The old man looks wonderingly at his pearl, then turns slowly to his wife.

Curtain.

66. THE SHADOW DRAGON

This fierce mythical monster is made from flat cardboard parts joined with paper fasteners. In the case of this shadow puppet, there are four control rods, two on the legs, one each on head and tail. The puppet could be simplified, with a single fixed rod to hold the dragon's body against the screen, a rod on head and tail, and the legs dangling free.

The dragon (or any other puppet) can be made to puff smoke with the addition of a fine rubber tube running up a fixed rod to the body and along behind the puppet to the mouth or nostrils. For a regular hand puppet, run the tubing up under the skirt to the head. Smoke can be puffed into the tube by mouth, or, if both the puppeteer's hands are occupied, with a foot bellows. Through similar use of tubing, puppets and props can be made to spout water and even confetti, as with the compressed air toy cannon opposite.

One last special trick: shadow waves can be made of silhouette cutouts that can be shifted back and forth one behind the other to simulate the rhythm of the seas.

These can simply be two cutouts held by hand, or can be mounted on swivels as shown. With some experimentation, they can even be animated mechanically and driven by a small electric motor.

Shadow Puppets

Shadow puppets have been popular for hundreds of years in China, India and Java (Indonesia). They are ideal for school, church and hospital puppetry, being cheap and easy to make and operate. For a shadow show all you need are some cut-out puppets, a screen and a strong light. The puppet material must be strong, but should be as thin as possible so as to cast a sharp shadow against the screen. Use stiff cardboard, sheet zinc or black sheet plastic. Be sure to put the heads of the paper fasteners on the side of the puppet that will face the screen. They will not snag the material. Settings cut from black paper can be removable themselves, or can be fixed permanently to screens which can be changed in the frame stage. Colored figures and backgrounds of colored plastic or colored oiled paper can be used to good effect.

A Shadow Stage

The screen material can be factory cotton, glazed chintz or oiled paper, stretched as tightly as possible on the frame. The screen should be set in its stand at a slight angle so that puppets can be rested against it. Use one strong light source, from above and behind, making sure that the shadows of the operator's heads are not cast on the screen. The stage can be as large as you wish, but you must have a strong enough light to cover the whole surface.

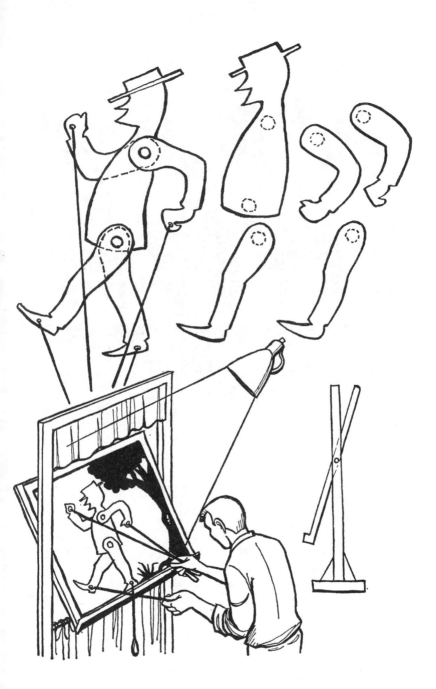

A Nativity Shadow Play

Shadow puppets are especially well adapted to such tableau presentations as the Story of the Nativity. The figures suggested here are not articulated, but they can be given movable joints like those of the shadow dragon. It is best to have two different scenes set up on separate screens that can be changed in the frame. A narrator should read the

story from the New Testament. Use recorded music or enlist
the help of the Sunday School choir. Suggested in the illustration are Mary and Joseph moving toward Bethlehem (67),
the shepherds tending their flocks (68), the Wise Men following the Star (69), the herald angel (70), the shepherds
kneeling at the stable (71), and the Wise Men coming
forward to adore the Christ Child (72).

Novelty Puppets

T HESE LAST two dozen designs include highly specialized comic and exotic puppets and some two-handed puppets. The puppeteer who has come this far is ready to exercise his own ingenuity, and so in most cases complete construction details are not given.

73. TROPICAL FLOWER

It looks like a potted plant, as shown above, but should some curious puppet put his head close to sniff its perfume, he will find himself quickly locked in a vise of quivering leaves. The pot is cardboard, open at the bottom. The paper leaves are attached to the fingers of a garden glove painted green, which the operator thrusts up through the pot, as shown opposite, C.

74, 75. THE LYNCH BROS.—

This song-and-dance team are sleeve puppets with articulated legs. The heads are of balsa wood, the hands made of foam rubber, carved with sharp scissors. The wooden legs are jointed at thigh and knee, and with some practice they can be made to tap-dance quite expertly along the playboard, see A.

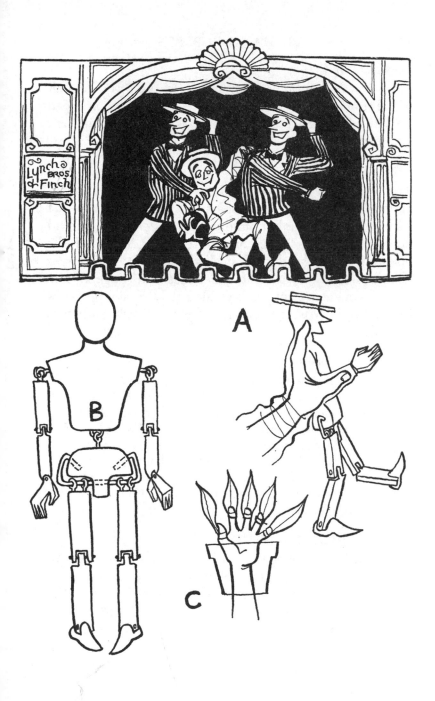

76. —AND FINCH

Finch is a fully articulated free doll, B, the tipsy member
of the trio, who is carried about by the other two; propped
up, he teeters, staggers and falls, hopelessly confusing their
vaudeville routines.

77. THE THING

This is a small cardboard box, painted black inside and
open at the bottom for the operator's hand. A loop on the
bottom fits the thumb, a loop on the underside of the lid
holds the fingers. By opening and closing his hand the
operator can make the lid snap like a mouth. Two eyes
dangle on a bit of black felt, which masks the fingers when
the lid is opened. Legs can be added. A black sleeve covers
the operator's wrist, and so the Thing must perform before
a black background.

Puppets and Music

The Thing is designed for use in presentation of a comic
novelty song in an LP album called *The Monster Rally*. However, the numbering and availability of recordings changes
so rapidly, no order numbers can be given in this book. It is
suggested that the puppeteer train himself to listen con-
tinually for musical possibilities and that he never pass up
the chance to buy or write down the name of a record he
thinks might be useful in the future. This includes background music for plays.

78. THE GASHOUSE 4 PLUS 1

Here is a five-member tailgate Dixie Land band. Two of
them are full hand puppets, the rest are mounted on
springs in the wagon bed and jiggle to the rhythm of the
music. The two front wheels are practical and can be
rolled along the playboard while the boys blow like fury.

79. WAHINI LOA

Like the Lynch Bros., this Hawaiian maiden has a black sleeve coming out of the middle of her back, through which the operator's arm passes. Her hips are attached to the torso by a single, angled swivel. The hips are weighted with lead, so that a twist of the operator's wrist causes them to swivel on their wire and set the cellophane skirt to weaving hula-hula style.

80. THE DANCING PALM TREE

Even the trees join in when Wahini Loa dances. The leaves can be made of paper or bought at a display store. The trunk is of painted canvas arranged around an angled center wire which is cranked from below to give the tree its weaving motion.

81. THE PURPLE PEOPLE EATER

Inspired by another song from the LP *The Monster Rally*, this one-handed, one-eyed, one-horned creature uses both the operator's hands, one inside the head, one inside the garden glove hand. The hand fingers the openings in the trumpet nose. The single eye is made from a large rubber ball. The nose, face, and eye socket are built of masking tape; the puppet is finished off with exotic cloth.

82. THE WEIRDS

Their heads are made of rubber balls cut in half and glued to the top and bottom of a universal hinged cardboard mouth. The heads are attached in a row to a wooden box frame, on which are painted the bodies and behind which the operator's hand hides to open and close their gaping mouths in chorus. They are especially good at caterwauling popular music.

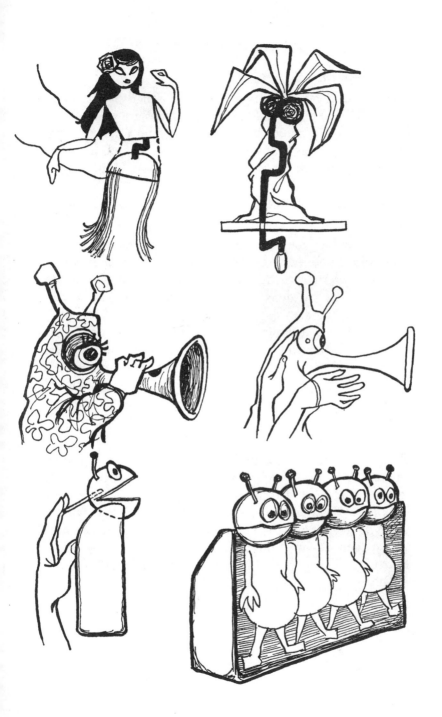

83. A HANDFUL OF ANGELS

These little finger puppets are made of rolled paper cones topped with wooden bead heads. The faces are painted on. The dresses are made of crepe paper, the arms of pipe cleaners, the wings of foil and the halos of aluminum wire. Slip one on each finger and you have a heavenly little host.

84. BIG CHIEF APPLESASS

Apples, carved and dried, make unusual and effective puppet heads, especially for such wrinkled faces as those of the old Chinese man and woman in the story of Suzume-San and for this leather-faced old Indian chief. Choose an apple with dry, dense meat; large crab apples are excellent. Break the skin in carving, but remove as little of it as possible; for instance, for the eyes, cut slits and press the edges of the skin inwards, rather than carving out the depression. Dry in good strong sunlight. The quicker the drying process, the less chance of rotting. A cardboard neck tube can be inserted either before or after carving.

85. OG-17

Here is an example of the many possibilities for puppet conversion to be found at the toy counter of your dime store. Og's head was a toy rocket ship that produced bubbles. Wooden eyes were glued on; a body with a teletype machine in the chest was added; the bubble tube was passed down through the cloth body, and we had a Martian who expressed himself by blowing bubbles out of his head.

86. PECOS PETE

Here is an old circus carpet clown trick reproduced in miniature for puppets. The body of the horse is made from a sheet of foam rubber bent in the form of a tunnel, with a hole in the top at the saddle position. This hole is small enough to hold tightly to the operator's wrist, which is also the waist of the puppet. The head of the horse can be overcast in papier-mâché or cut out in silhouette from cardboard; the tail is unraveled twine. False paper legs are added at the sides. Thus any puppet can be put astride a horse by simply slipping it on as you slip on a bracelet.

87. LIGHTNIN' BUG

His chest is made of corduroy, his shell is overcast papier-mâché. His cut-out cardboard hands are suspended at the ends of wiggly coil spring arms. The operator's hand fits into his mouth to open and close it. Small electric bulbs are attached to the ends of his feelers. Their wires run down through his body to a battery and push button, so that they can be made to blink on and off.

88. HUFF 'N PUFF

This parakeet couple can be operated with one hand. The cast papier-mâché or plastic wood heads rest loosely in the shoulders and are fixed to rods which run down the perch to two wheels below. The wheels can be turned by the operator's thumb, thus turning the heads from side to side. The beaks are movable and are operated by thin wires running down the perch and looped at the ends to fit the operator's first and fourth fingers. Which is all just to show you how complicated rod puppets can get.

89. THE MAESTRO

His head is a large ball of styro-foam with ping pong ball
eyes inserted, a cardboard nose glued in place and a crepe
hair wig flowing wildly. The body is a large, loosely draped
cloth, hiding the operator, who holds the head aloft with
one hand and directs the orchestra with the other.

2-Hand Puppets

They are fun to operate and very effective, especially
when the second hand is actually used as a hand, usually
clad in a white dress or garden glove. One problem which
arises is, "Where is the puppet's other hand?" The question
can be avoided by draping heavily to suggest that the second
hand is concealed in the folds of a dress or cape, as with
the Maestro, or by adding a scarf on one side, as in the case
of Hush Columbo.

90, 91. THE WORMS

They are made from two green or rose-colored socks. They argue endlessly over whether or not they are the two ends of the same worm and if so, as to which of them is the nether end!

92. HUSH COLUMBO

His head is of cast papier-mâché with ping-pong eyeballs, movable if you wish. His shell is cast papier-mâché. Masking must be draped loosely down between the narrow space between the puppet and the operator, who is directly behind the puppet.

93. HAND AND MOUF

This luminous hand and mouth float before a black background, pantomiming to Al Jolson recordings. The mouth
is a doughnut-shaped roll of white cloth sewed to the ends
of the fingers of a black glove attached to a black sleeve.
The hand is a white garden or dress glove attached to a
black sleeve. Black velvet is best for sleeves and background, as it absorbs light well and sets off the white ob-
jects. Hand and Mouf have been used successfully on TV.

Puppets on TV

Television offers many technical advantages that are not
found in live puppet theater. For instance, there is an electronic process called "blanking down" which increases the
light contrast in the TV picture so that Hand and Mouf can
be made to float in darkness with absolutely no sign of
human aid. TV offers all the advantages of movies: the
opportunity to change from scene to scene instantaneously,
close-up pictures of the puppets, electronic double images,
etc. Puppets need not be large for television, as the camera
can get close enough to make them loom big as life.

A TV Stage

The television puppet stage can be as long as wished,
because the picture can be quickly changed from a camera
at one end of the stage to a camera at the other. The only
limitation is the puppeteer's ability to gallop from scene to
scene. Monitor sets should be positioned back stage, so that
the operator can see exactly what kind of a picture of his
puppets is being shown. When doing a show for TV, get as
much practice as you can with the use of these monitor sets.
It takes time to get used to the fact that you are seeing your
puppet *backwards;* that is, the puppet on your left hand is
on the right of the TV screen.

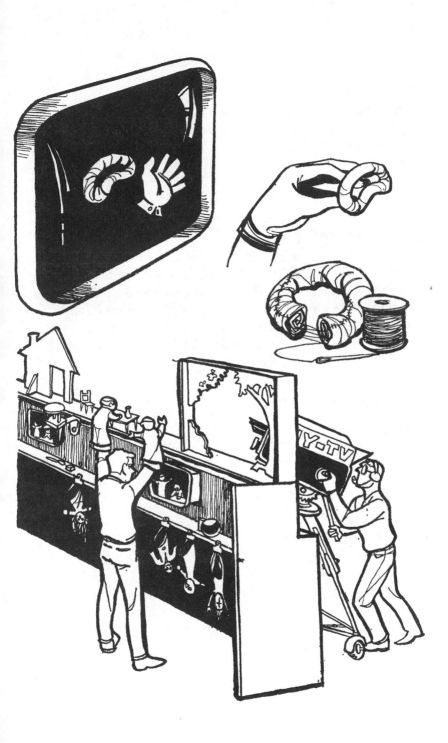

Black Light

The fluorescent paints and cloth and special lamps of theatrical "black light" are expensive, but can be very effective in live puppet presentations. There are special cloth materials from which Hand and Mouf can be made. There are colored liquid and spray paints with which puppet costumes and faces can be made to glow in the dark.

94, 95. TOP HAT AND FEATHER BOA

An opera hat and a long feather boa can be sprayed with fluorescent paints and made to dance with one another, the boa weaving sinuously up and down and around the trembling, bashful hat. Other props can be quite fantastic under black light. A luminescent trombone could play so vigorously that it loses its slide and has to chase it here and there about the stage.

96. CECELIA OSTRICH

Her thick-lashed eyes are articulated in a round papier-mâché head. Her neck consists of most of the operator's arm enclosed in a tight jersey sleeve. Her tail of real ostrich plumes is held in the operator's other hand and undulates prettily as she stalks along.

97. SCRIBBLES McDIBBLE

His latex nose hangs over the top edge of his slate and is waggled by the operator's right hand. His left hand, which is also the operator's left hand reaches around the drawing board and draws pictures and writes messages. The right hand holding the edge of the board is a false hand of papier-mâché.

98. JUMBO

Here is a 2-handed elephant in two pieces, front and back. His head is made of cloth over a papier-mâché shell, with the trunk weighted to give it an elephantine swing. The body is made of gray cloth over two sections constructed of cardboard. He does a lumbering dance to slow music, only to discover that his back end has left him and is dancing independently. His efforts to fit himself back together properly can be very comic.

99. HOT DOG

This stretchy 2-handed pup is made of brown plush or velvet, with a papier-mâché head overlaid with cloth, only the nose and eyes left exposed to be painted. The operator's right hand fits into the puppet's head and moves the hinged mouth. The left hand fits into the back end, first finger extended into the tail to make it wag. The body is made of one of the metal coil toys called "slinkys" and is slung between the two ends and covered with a sheath of matching brown velvet. The body can be made to expand or retract; the dog can even turn around upon himself.

100. ANNA CONDA

Her skeleton is one of the more slender slinkys. (They are often found as a part of other toys.) Her head is made of a sock, her body of a tube of painted yellow velvet. She is operated with two hands, one inside the head and masked with a black sleeve, the other controlling the rod attached to her tail.

101. MARK TWAIN

At one time or another the author has made all of the
puppets in this book, with the exception of this one, which
is a suggested modern version of the large articulated
puppets of Osaka, Japan. The Osaka puppets are manipu-
lated by as many as three people standing behind the
puppet. The operators are in full view of the audience,
but they wear dark clothing and dark hoods over their
heads. The voices of the Osaka puppets come from offstage, but in this case one of the operators would probably
provide the voice for Mark Twain, who, come to life on
the puppet stage, would once again spin out his wondrous
and comic yarns.

Puppets or Marionettes?

PUPPET is the family name and includes both hand puppets and marionettes. Marionettes are worked by threads or wires from above. They are agile and complete creatures and can dance and leap and even fly, but they have their drawbacks. They are more complicated and expensive to make than most hand puppets, and when they walk they either seem to be sitting on air or they trip across the stage on tip-toes.

The hand puppet is earthbound and he often has no legs, but he has the great advantage of direct, convincing action. A good performer can move him so that the subtlest movement has just the right shade of meaning. He is inexpensive to make; he has no strings to tangle; and children love him best for the right reason: he is more nearly flesh and blood and living spirit.

For this book we have considered all those puppets that are operated from below or behind, but not from above, and have called them Hand Puppets. The English call them Fist Puppets or Mitten Puppets, the French *Guignols*, the Italians *Burattini*, the Germans *Handpuppen, Kasperlpuppen,* or *Kasperlfiguren*.

In any language they are a joy, and they offer you a new glimpse of the world of yourself. Choose a puppet, gather your materials and begin!

Index